The JUMBO BOOK of
PAPER
Crafts

Written by Amanda Lewis

Illustrated by Jane Kurisu

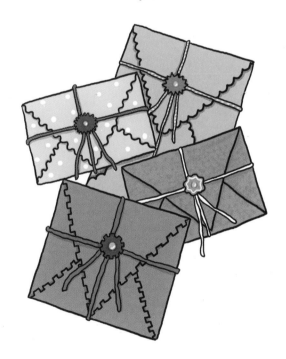

Kids Can Press

Contents

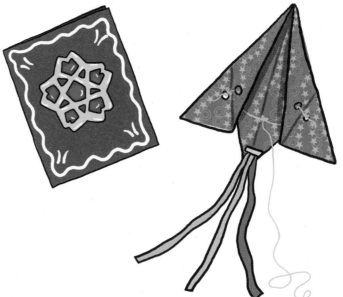

Introduction

Ever since the Chinese mashed up rags and old fishing nets to make paper, it's been one of the most important and useful inventions in the world! For more than 2000 years, paper has been used for cooking, wrapping and building, for making clothing, furniture and insulation. And of course it's perfect for writing on and making art with. Paper is strong, easy to use and inexpensive. This book will give you lots of ideas for how to use paper to create gifts, toys, jewelry, books, decorations, cards — there's no end to the wonderful things you can make with paper!

PAPERS

One of the best things about making paper crafts is finding interesting papers to use. The projects in this book work best if you make them with the paper that's suggested in the instructions. Most of these papers are available at craft, art or stationery supply stores.

Bond Paper: This is regular 22 cm x 27 cm (8½ in. x 11 in.) paper. You can get it in white or a rainbow of colors.

Art Paper: Art paper comes in different thicknesses and sizes. It is usually sold by the sheet in lots of colors and textures.

Heavy Art Paper or Card Stock: A heavy paper should be thicker than a piece of bond paper, but not so thick that it can't fold. Papers such as Canson or other brand names work well.

Japanese Paper: Japanese paper has long fibers, so it doesn't break when folded. It comes in beautiful and unusual colors and designs.

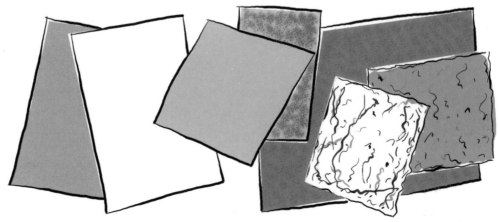

Origami Paper: Origami paper comes in different sizes, but the most common is 15 cm x 15 cm (6 in. x 6 in.). You'll find it in packages of single- or double-sided colors, metal foil or patterned.

Wrapping Paper or Decorative Paper: Wrapping paper is useful for more than wrapping gifts! Find some that is strong — the paper in rolls of inexpensive Christmas wrap tears too easily. For many projects you can reuse wrapping paper from a present you received. Stationery stores sell single sheets of decorative paper that works as well.

Wallpaper: You can make many crafts from scraps of unused wallpaper. Stores that sell wallpaper sometimes give away old pattern books filled with great pieces of paper.

Construction Paper: Construction paper comes in lots of interesting colors, patterns and textures. It is great for some projects in this book. But construction paper fades quickly if left out in the light. It also has very short fibers, so it tears easily along fold lines. Don't substitute it for other papers.

Tissue Paper: You can get large sheets of tissue paper in terrific colors.

Crepe Paper: Use crepe-paper party streamers for the crafts in this book. They are available in lots of colors and can be found at grocery or dollar stores.

Matboard: Matboard is used to frame pictures and photographs. If you ask at a framing or photography store, they might give you some scraps. Most projects use only very small pieces. You can also buy pieces of matboard at craft or art supply stores.

Thin Cardboard: Some projects use thin cardboard. Use old cereal or cracker boxes.

◨ WORKING WITH PAPER

Some techniques are useful to know when making the projects in this book. These "tricks of the trade" will make your paper crafts work really well.

Scoring and Folding: The more accurately you fold, the better your craft will look. Scoring your paper helps you fold it more easily. To score, lay a ruler along the line where you want your paper to fold. Press down on the ruler to hold it in place. Run a small knitting needle, an old ballpoint pen (with no ink left) or a Popsicle stick along the ruler. The impression you make on the paper is the score line. You can then fold accurately along this line.

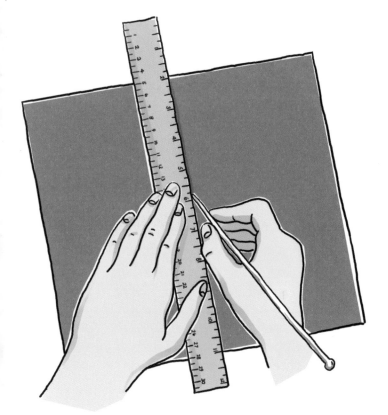

Making Folds Crisp and Sharp: After you have scored and folded your paper, it's a good idea to make the folds crisp and sharp. Press down firmly on your paper to keep it in place, and gently run the side of a pencil or plastic ruler from the middle of the fold out to each side.

Valley and Mountain Folds: When you look sideways at a folded piece of paper, a fold that goes down is called a valley. A fold that goes up is called a mountain. To reverse a fold, make it go in the opposite direction.

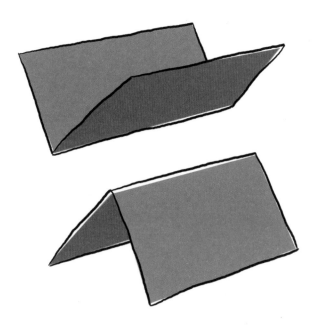

Gluing: The projects in this book use either a glue stick or white craft glue. When you are gluing, place the paper face down on newspaper, hold it steady and spread the glue from the center to the outer edge. This will keep your paper from crumpling and getting glue on the wrong side.

Pressing: Sometimes glued paper should be pressed so that it will dry flat. Put glued papers between sheets of wax paper to keep them from sticking to anything. Put a stack of heavy books on top to press the papers flat until they dry.

Cutting: You'll need scissors and an X-Acto or craft knife. X-Acto knives often make the best cuts on paper. Always ask an adult to help you use one. Put a cutting board under your paper when you use an X-Acto knife.

Covering: You may want to cover some of your projects with a sealer to make them strong and shiny. Use an acrylic varnish or water-soluble sealer such as Podge, Podgy, Mod Podge or Podgecoat, available at craft supply stores.

Measuring: The measurements in this book are given in both metric and imperial. They differ slightly, so choose one system and use it for the entire project.

Paper Folding

You can make lots of unusual toys, gifts, cards, books, jewelry and decorations simply by folding paper! The Japanese art of paper folding is called origami. You can get special origami papers that work perfectly for many of these projects. They are strong and hold their folds well. All of these folded crafts use very few materials other than paper, and most are quick and easy to make.

TIPS:

Many projects in this section will work fine with bond paper, magazine paper or wrapping paper, but not with construction paper. It doesn't hold folds well.

Look for interesting papers to show off your folds. Gold and silver metallic wrapping paper makes a spectacular effect. Patterned origami paper gives your projects unique designs.

See page 8 for tips on scoring, folding and sharpening folds. The more carefully you fold, the better your crafts will look.

Bell Chime

Hang this ornament beside your bedroom door, and people can ring it gently to get your attention. If you attach it to your door, it will ring whenever the door opens or closes.

◣ You will need:

- 8 squares of wrapping paper, 20 cm x 20 cm (8 in. x 8 in.)
- yarn
- 8 pieces of bond paper, 4 cm x 15 cm (1½ in. x 6 in.)
- string or cord, 4 m (13 ft.) long
- a small bell
- scissors

1 Place a wrapping paper square face down. Fold it in half diagonally, open it and repeat with the other diagonal.

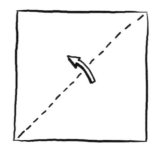

2 Turn the paper over. Fold it in half, open it and repeat in the other direction.

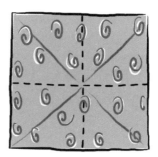

3 Press up on the center point. Push in valley folds (page 8) so that you have a series of folded triangles.

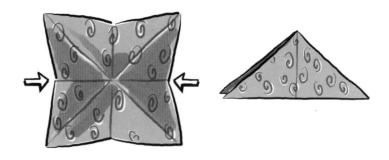

4 Repeat steps 1 to 3 with the remaining wrapping paper squares.

5 Fold the yarn in half. Make a double knot about 15 cm (6 in.) from the folded end.

6 Cut off the tip of the folded top of one triangular paper. Open the paper out flat. Pull the cut ends of the yarn through the hole from the top. Push the paper up to the knot in the yarn.

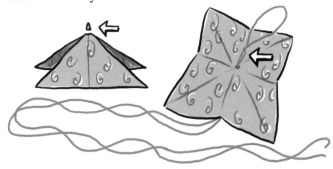

7 Fold a piece of bond paper in half four times. Wind the yarn around this paper, about 5 cm (2 in.) from the hole in the triangular paper, and tie it into a knot. Pull tight and tie a second knot.

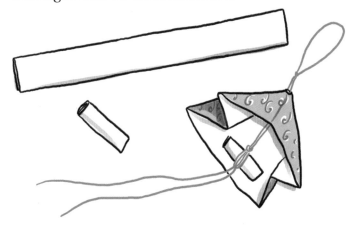

8 Repeat step 6, pushing the triangular paper up to stay 8 cm (3 in.) from the knotted paper.

9 Repeat step 7. Continue adding triangles and knotted papers until you have added all the pieces.

10 Trim the yarn to about 20 cm (8 in.) from the last knotted paper. Tie the bell to the end. Re-press all folds to sharpen them.

Puffy Stars

Use strips of magazine or wrapping paper to make these fun little stars. Hang them in a window or use them for the mobile on the next page. Longer and wider strips make bigger stars.

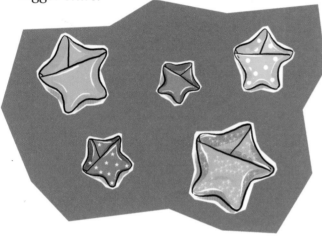

◤ You will need:

- a strip of paper for each star, 22 cm x 1 cm (8½ in. x ½ in.)
- needle and thin nylon or beading thread
- scissors

1 Tie one end of the paper in a knot. Pull the paper so that the sides of the knot are even. Press the knot flat. Trim the short end of the paper to match the edge of the knot.

2 Fold the long end over the knot then over the trimmed end and press it to the back.

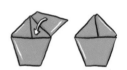

3 Fold the paper to the front again. It will naturally fold at an angle across each side. Continue to fold around and around the paper.

4 When you reach the end of the paper, tuck it into a fold.

5 Hold the knot with a finger on each side. Using your other hand, press inward to puff out the star and give it its shape. Repeat to make other stars.

6 To hang your star, thread a needle and sew from the bottom of the star up through the opposite point. Leaving a small loop at the top, go down through the same holes. Knot the thread together at the bottom. Trim the thread.

Mobile

▶ You will need:

- 5 wooden dowels, 0.25 cm (⅛ in.) in diameter and 20 cm (8 in.) long
- scissors, thin nylon or beading thread

1 Cut three long threads, 30 cm (12 in.). Cut six medium threads, 25 cm (10 in.). Cut two short threads, 18 cm (7 in.).

2 Tie one long and one short piece of thread to each end of a dowel.

3 Tie the end of each thread to the middle of another dowel.

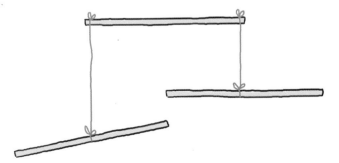

4 Tie one long and one short piece of thread to each end of the dowel that is tied to the short thread. Repeat step 3.

5 Tie a medium thread at each end of the three dowels. Tie on puffy stars or other paper crafts.

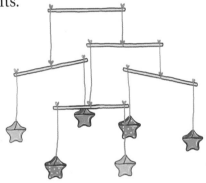

6 To hang your mobile, tie the last long thread in the middle of the first dowel. Balance the mobile by sliding the strings until the dowels hang straight.

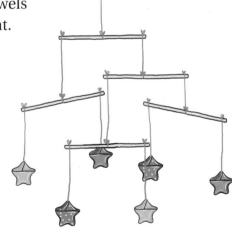

Metallic Sunburst

Hang this sunburst pattern as a decoration or use it as an elegant round fan.

◢ You will need:

- a piece of metallic wrapping paper, 23 cm x 60 cm (9 in. x 24 in.)
- 2 squares of contrasting heavy paper, 18 cm x 18 cm (7 in. x 7 in.)
- stapler, scissors, glue stick, paper clips or clothespins

1 Make a 2.5 cm (1 in.) fold on the short end of the metallic paper. Turn it over and fold in the other direction. Keep folding from one side to the other, matching the previous fold, until you reach the end. The last fold may not be exactly the same size as the others.

2 Fold the folded strip in half. Press. Open it and staple across the middle, once from each side.

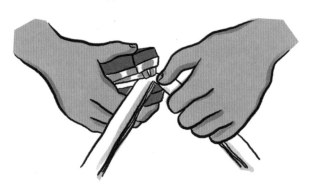

3 Holding the strip together, cut out small shapes along fold lines.

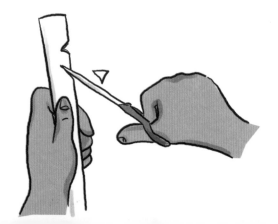

4 Open the strip into a fan shape. Spread glue along one folded side. Fold the fan in half and press the glued edges together. Hold it together with paper clips until dry.

7 Spread glue along the unglued sides of the fan. Press a handle on each side, leaving a 0.5 cm (¼ in.) gap in the center. Hold together with paper clips until dry, then open your sunburst.

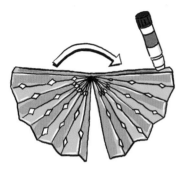

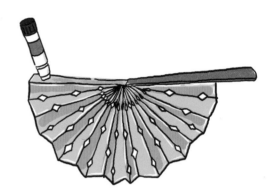

5 To make a handle, fold over 2.5 cm (1 in.) on one of your heavy paper squares. Fold over again, folding the paper over itself. Keep folding until you reach the end.

◼ Other Ideas:

Make a delicate sunburst with tissue paper. Use two or three pieces of tissue on top of each other for the fan and heavy paper for the handles.

6 Spread glue along the last fold and press it in place. Hold it together with paper clips to dry. Repeat for a second handle.

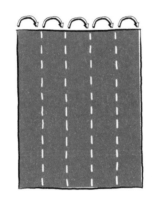

17

Folded Card

This project turns a piece of paper into a surprising card. You can photocopy it onto colored paper to give as a special gift. Make a cover, and you can turn your card into a small book.

◢ You will need:

- a piece of bond paper,
  22 cm x 27 cm (8½ in. x 11 in.)
- a piece of decorative paper,
  22 cm x 27 cm (8½ in. x 11 in.), optional
- pencil, scissors, ruler

1 Fold the bond paper in half lengthwise. Open it. Fold in half widthwise. Open it.

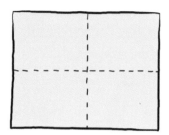

2 Fold the sides in to meet the middle fold. Open the paper flat.

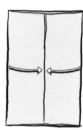

3 Use a pencil to lightly number the pages as shown.

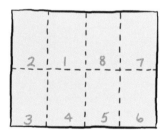

4 Write, draw or collage (page 120) a message or story onto the pages, leaving pages 1 and 8 blank. Keep the fold at the top of each page. Photocopy the finished paper if you want to make copies.

5 Cut the middle fold between pages 1 and 8 to the center line, as shown. Cut along the center fold line between pages 1 and 4 and pages 5 and 8, as shown. You should have a T-shaped cut.

6 Lift the paper so that the fold is at the top. Push the end sections into the middle. Lay the folded sections on top of each other and reverse the folds of the last two sections so that they close over the card. Write or draw on the front and back.

7 To make a cover, score (page 8) and fold over a 5.5 cm (2⅛ in.) margin along the top and a 5 cm (2 in.) margin along the bottom of the decorative paper.

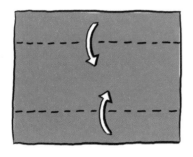

8 Score and fold over a 7 cm (2¾ in.) margin along one side and a 6.5 cm (2½ in.) margin along the other. Open them.

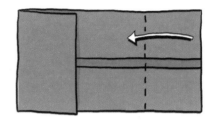

9 Measure 7 cm (2¾ in.) from each side fold. You should have a small spine (back edge) for your cover, about 0.5 cm (¼ in.) wide, down the center of the paper. Score and fold along these lines.

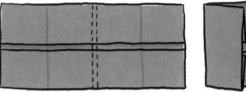 

10 Place the folded card in the center of the cover. Slide pages 1 and 8 into the end sections of the cover.

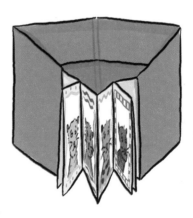

Kite

This simple paper kite is easy to launch by yourself, and it flies well with just a little wind.

◣ You will need:

- a square of decorative paper,
  22 cm x 22 cm (8½ in. x 8½ in.)

- 3 strips of tissue paper, 1 cm x 90 cm (½ in. x 36 in.)
  — you may have to tape pieces together for length

- a spool of thin nylon or beading thread

- scissors, tape, hole punch

1 Fold the square paper in half diagonally.

2 Fold the top right corner down so that one side meets the fold.

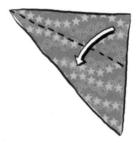 

3 Fold the corner back up so that the side meets the fold.

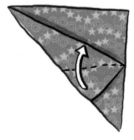 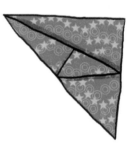

4 Turn the paper over and repeat steps 2 and 3. Sharpen all folds (page 8).

5 Cut off the folded corner tip.

6 Put a 2 cm (¾ in.) piece of tape over the outer diagonal fold 1 cm (½ in.) from the corner, as shown. Place a second piece of tape over top. Punch a hole through both layers. Repeat on the other side.

7 Cut a 30 cm (12 in.) piece of thread. With the middle of the paper facing you as a mountain fold (page 8), tie the thread through the holes.

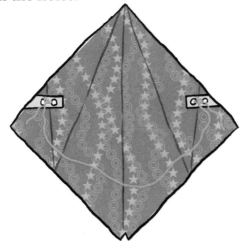

8 Tape the strips of tissue paper to the wide end of the kite.

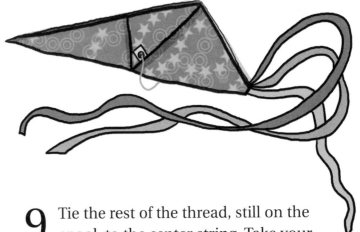

9 Tie the rest of the thread, still on the spool, to the center string. Take your kite out when there is a good breeze. Hold it high to feel the wind, and slowly run away from it. Let out the string as the kite catches in the air.

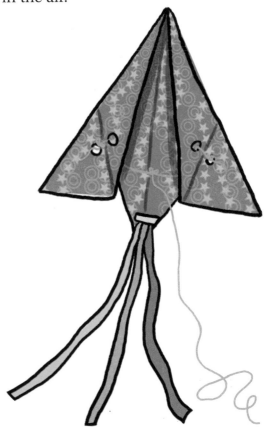

Boats

You can make these boats a little water-resistant by coloring the paper heavily with wax crayons before you fold it. Or make your boats from foil origami paper. It looks great and also helps them last longer in the water. Use a 15 cm x 15 cm (6 in. x 6 in.) square of paper for each boat.

SIMPLE BOAT

1 Fold the square of paper in half. With the fold at the bottom, fold the lower corners halfway up, making the sides parallel with the top of the boat.

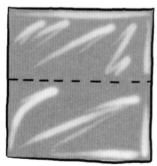

2 Fold the front section down to meet the top of the folded corners. Fold it over again.

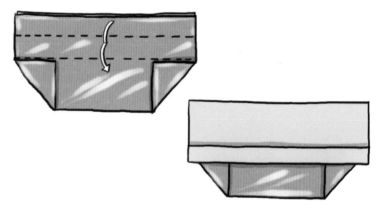

3 Turn the paper over and fold the top section down to match the front.

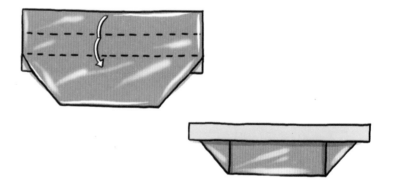

4 Open the boat and gently flatten the base.

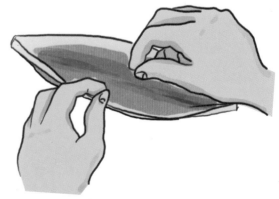

◪ CATAMARAN BOAT

1 Fold the square in half diagonally. Open it. Repeat with the other diagonal. Open it.

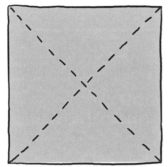

2 Fold all the corners in to the middle.

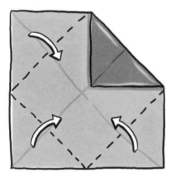

3 Turn the paper over. Fold two opposite corners in to meet at the center.

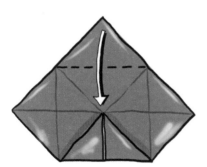

4 Turn the paper over. Fold the two remaining corners in to meet at the center.

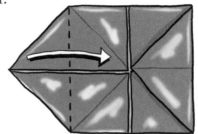

5 Pull a corner from underneath the right triangle, stretching it down. Hold the left side closed.

6 Repeat this process with the remaining three corners.

7 Fold the two halves down, side by side. Press the fold and gently open the boat.

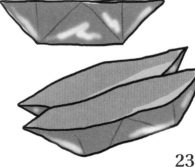

Planes

◆ SIMPLE AIRPLANE

This adjustable airplane flies really well.

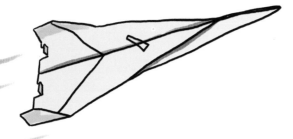

◆ You will need:

- a piece of bond paper,
  22 cm x 27 cm (8½ in. x 11 in.)
- ruler, pencil, tape, scissors

1 Fold the paper in half lengthwise. Open it. Fold the top corners in to the center.

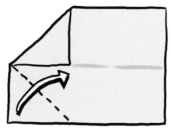

2 Fold the new corners in to meet at the center, as shown.

3 Fold in half along the fold line.

4 Measure a 3 cm (1¼ in.) strip on each wing along the lower edge of the plane. Score (page 8) and fold each wing along this line.

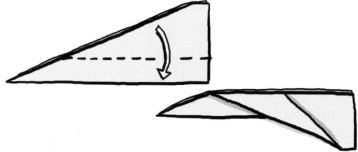

5 Fold up a 2 cm (¾ in.) flap at the tip of each wing.

6 Hold the plane by the base. Open the side flaps out horizontally. Tape them together at the top.

7 Cut flaps into the tail of the wings by making two 1 cm (½ in.) slits on each wing, approximately 1 cm (½ in.) from the center fold. Fold these flaps up.

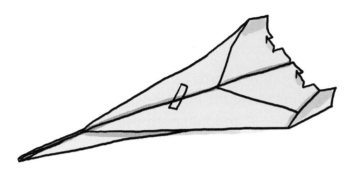

8 Test fly your plane. If it nosedives, adjust the back flaps higher. Make your plane roll by putting one flap up and the other down.

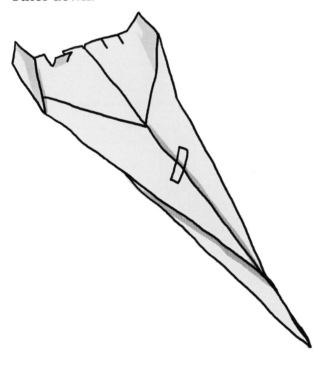

GLIDER

You will need:

- a piece of bond paper, 13 cm x 27 cm (5 in. x 11 in.)
- a piece of bond paper, 2.5 cm x 27 cm (1 in. x 11 in.)
- a piece of bond paper, 2.5 cm x 13 cm (1 in. x 5 in.)
- tape

1 Roll the large paper into a cylinder about 1 cm (½ in.) in diameter. Tape along the join to hold it in place.

2 Make a circle with each of the other papers, holding them together with tape.

3 Attach a circle to one end of the cylinder by laying it on top of the join and taping. Repeat with the other circle.

4 Fly your plane with the small circle at the front. If the plane nosedives, move the large circle forward a bit. If it wobbles, move the small circle back a bit.

Flying Saucer

This paper disk flies like a whirling Frisbee. Make it with fluorescent or metallic paper and decorate the sides to look like a UFO.

◤ You will need:

- 5 squares of bond paper, 22 cm x 22 cm (8½ in. x 8½ in.)
- stickers or stamps, markers (optional)
- tape, pencil, ruler

1 Fold a square of paper in half. With the fold at the top, fold each corner down to meet at the middle of the unfolded base.

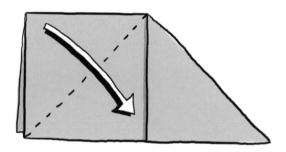

2 Open one corner, then refold it as shown so that the corner meets the inside of the diagonal fold. Flatten it.

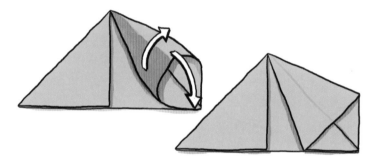

3 Repeat with each square.

4 Push the pointed end of one paper all the way into the folded pocket of another. Hold it in place with tape, as shown.

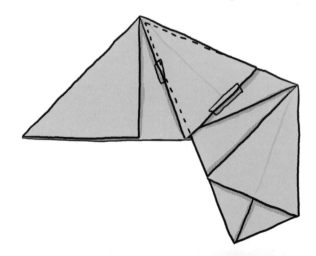

5 Repeat with the other three pieces, going in a circle to form a disk. When you push the last piece in, it will feel as if it doesn't fit, and the edge of the disk will start to curl up. That's what you want. Tape it in place. Your disk should be almost like a bowl with a hole in the middle.

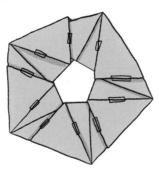

6 Turn the disk over. Tape down the backs of the papers.

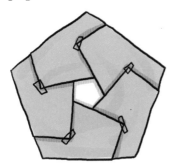

7 Make a mark 7.5 cm (3 in.) from one point. Fold the point to touch this mark. Repeat with each point.

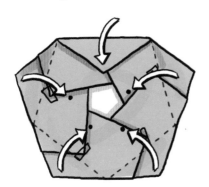

8 Open the points so that they stand up. Decorate with stickers, stamps or drawings, if you like.

9 To fly the saucer, hold it with the points facing up and let it go with a flick of the wrist.

27

Diary Necklace

This tiny sewn book attached to a chain or cord is the perfect place to record your special thoughts or wishes.

◆ You will need:

- 6 pieces of bond paper, 3 cm x 6.5 cm (1¼ in. x 2½ in.)

- a piece of art or wallpaper, 4 cm x 20 cm (1½ in. x 7½ in.)

- a jewelry ring

- thin chain, decorative cord or leather lace

- scissors, ruler, pencil, bulldog clip or clothespin, cutting board, small nail, hammer (optional), strong needle and thread

- thin ribbon (optional)

1 Fold the pieces of bond paper in half widthwise. Place one inside the other.

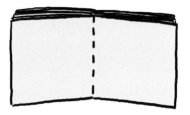

2 Fold the art paper into 4 cm (1½ in.) sections as shown.

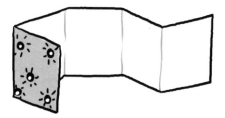

3 Trim off 0.25 cm (⅛ in.) from the inside of the first folded section.

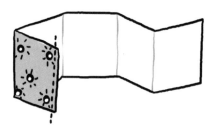

4 With the right side of the art paper facing you, place the folded papers on the first section. Match the folds and position the papers in the center. Use a bulldog clip to hold in place.

5 Fold the third and fourth sections back over the first and second. Fold the last section around to cover the first section. The cover should now be wrapped over itself. Adjust the clip to hold the papers and cover in place.

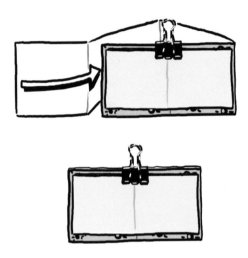

6 Put the book on the cutting board. Make three evenly spaced holes along the fold by having an adult help you to push or hammer the nail through the papers.

7 Thread the needle with 40 cm (16 in.) of thread, doubling it and making a double knot about 8 cm (3 in.) from the end.

8 Sew from the back, going through the middle hole first. Then go through the top hole from the front to the back. String on the jewelry ring. Skip the middle hole and go through the bottom hole. Finish by going through the center hole from the front to the back. Gently pull the thread tight. Go through the jewelry ring again and knot the ends together. Knot it twice and trim any excess thread.

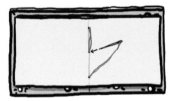

9 Thread the chain through the ring. Tie the book closed with a thin ribbon, if you like, slipping the ribbon through the stitching at the back.

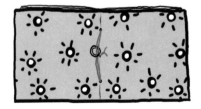

Butterfly

This simple ornament, made with magazine paper, looks as beautiful as if it were made with the finest decorative paper. Liven up your room by putting several on a wall or door.

◣ You will need:

- a square of magazine paper, 16 cm x 16 cm (6½ in. x 6½ in.)
- a piece of magazine paper 26 cm x 19 cm (10½ in. x 7½ in.)
- pipe cleaner
- scissors

1 Fold the square in half diagonally. Fold the bottom up 1 cm (½ in.). Turn the paper over. Fold over 1 cm (½ in.). Turn. Continue folding and turning until you reach the top.

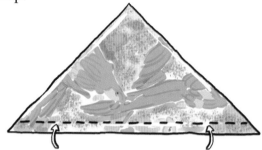

2 Open the square. Starting from the middle fold as a valley fold, reverse the next fold to be a mountain fold (page 8). Reverse all the folds on that side of the square so that you have a series of mountain and valley folds.

3 Cut the other piece of magazine paper into a shape as shown. Make the base 26 cm (10½ in.) and the height 19 cm (7½ in.).

4 Fold over 1 cm (½ in.) on the base of the shaped piece. Turn and fold over 1 cm (½ in.). Continue turning and folding until you reach the end.

5 With both pieces folded into accordions, pinch them in the middle and hold them closed.

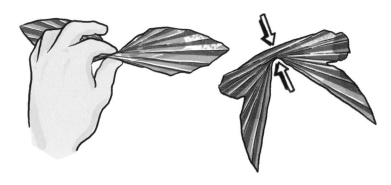

6 Place the first piece on top of the second, matching the middles. Wind the pipe cleaner around the middle, twisting it to hold the sections together. Curl the ends of the pipe cleaner into antennae. Gently stretch the papers open.

Other Ideas:

Make tiny butterflies out of smaller pieces of paper, 4 cm x 4 cm (1½ in. x 1½ in.) and 6.5 cm x 3 cm (2½ in. x 1¼ in.). Use a twist tie to attach them. Put the butterflies on a mobile (page 15), make them into earrings (page 145), add them to a card box (page 42), or glue them onto a barrette form (page 144) or gift card.

Good Luck Crane

This bird is supposed to bring you good luck. Enclose it in a letter, hang it from your window, or make a flock for a mobile (page 15).

You will need:

- a square of origami paper
- needle and thread, scissors

1 Fold the paper in half diagonally. Fold it in half diagonally again.

2 Turn the paper so that the long edge is at the bottom and the open sides are on the right. Open the top right corner, folding it over to the left, creating a square as you press corner to corner.

3 Flip the paper over and repeat on the other side, reversing the diagonal fold into a valley fold (page 8). You should now have two squares on top of each other.

4 Turn the paper so that the folded point is at the top. Fold the lower sides in to touch the center fold. Fold the top corner down over the edges. Open all of these folds.

5 Lift the bottom corner of the top layer. Open it, folding the sides over along the fold lines and meeting them in the center.

6 Turn the paper over and repeat steps 4 and 5.

7 Fold the corners of the top layer in to meet at the center. Turn the paper over and repeat on the other side.

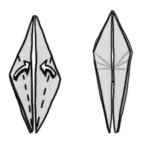

8 Fold one lower section out at an angle as shown. Unfold. Repeat with the other section.

9 Open the side folds and bring the lower section to the inside, folding along the fold line and reversing the fold. Repeat with the second section.

10 Fold down the top part of one of the pointed sections to create a head.

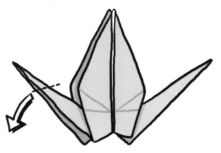

11 Fold down and open the wings. Puff out the body by blowing in the hole at the bottom of the crane.

12 To hang your crane, thread a needle and make a large knot at the end. Push the needle up through the hole at the bottom of the crane and out the top of the body. Take the needle off and cut the thread to the desired length.

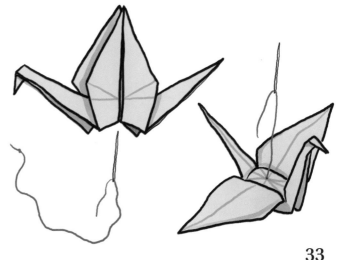

33

Wish Wheel

Some people believe that prayers or wishes will be answered if the words are carried away by the wind. Write your wishes inside this wish wheel and see if they come true.

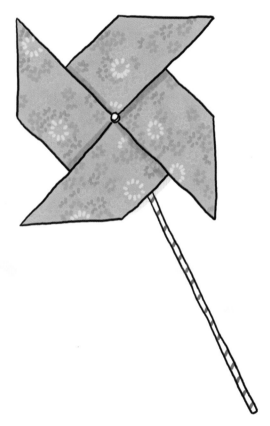

You will need:

- a square of wrapping or large origami paper, 30 cm x 30 cm (12 in. x 12 in.)
- a push pin
- a plastic straw or sturdy stick
- a pen or pencil

1 Fold the paper in half in both directions, opening after each fold. Fold it in half diagonally in both directions. Open.

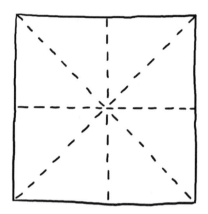

2 Fold a side in to meet the middle fold. Open. Repeat with all four sides.

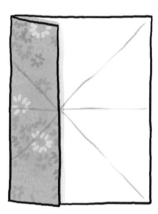

3 Turn the paper over. Fold each corner in to meet at the center. Write your wishes on these triangles.

4 Open all the folds. Turn the paper over. Fold the top and bottom in to meet in the center.

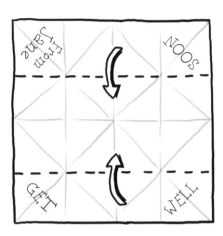

5 Push the middle of the side in to the center, letting the corners open out as shown. Repeat with the other side.

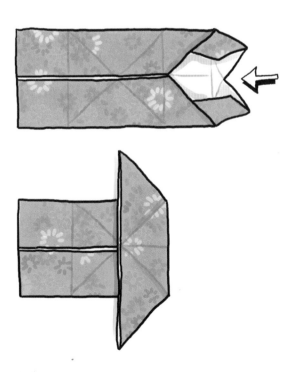

6 Fold the top right corner over to the side. Fold the bottom left corner over to the side. Press flat.

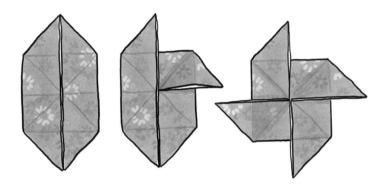

7 Push the push pin into the center and into the straw or stick. Leave it loose so that the wheel will easily spin. Take it outside on a sunny, windy day and let the wind carry your wishes away.

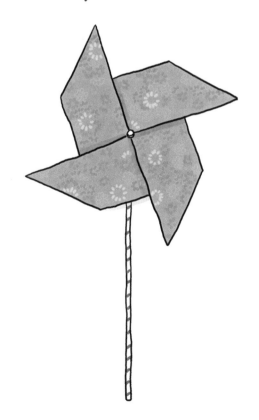

Kimono

This little kimono can be hung as an ornament or glued to a gift card. Paper that has a pattern will look more like fabric when your kimono is finished.

 You will need:

- a piece of origami or wrapping paper, 5 cm x 15 cm (2 in. x 6 in.)
- glue stick (optional)
- strong thread, 38 cm (15 in.) long
- toothpick
- pencil, ruler

1 Place the paper lengthwise, face down. Fold over 0.5 cm (¼ in.) of the top edge. Fold the edge over again.

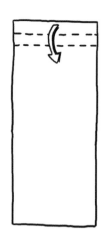

2 Turn the paper over. Fold it in half lengthwise. Open it. Fold the top left corner down to meet the center fold. Fold the right corner down to meet the fold.

3 Lightly mark a line 8.5 cm (3¾ in.) from the bottom. Fold the top to the back along this line. Flip the paper over and turn it so the fold is at the bottom.

4 Lightly mark a line 3.5 cm (1¾ in.) from the unfolded edge of the paper. Fold back along this line.

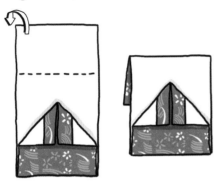

5 Fold both side sections in to meet the sides of the collar line. Open out both short side sections, flattening the tops into triangles, as shown.

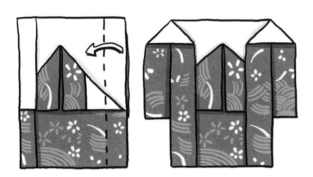

6 Fold back the top behind the collar, folding it even with the fold in the collar section (approximately 1 cm [½ in.]).

7 To hang your kimono, spread glue along the edge of the back folded flap. Tie the middle of the thread to the middle of the toothpick. Place the toothpick under the flap. Pull each end of the thread to a side of the kimono. Press the flap down.

8 Dab glue onto the back of the large flap and press down. Tie the ends of thread together and hang.

◤ Other Ideas:

● Turn your kimono into a fancy pin. After step 6, use spray varnish or Podge to make your kimono sturdy. Use white glue to attach a jewelry pin to the back.

● Glue a kimono onto a gift card or on top of a gift box (page 44) for a unique present. Kimonos also make a beautiful mobile (page 15).

Fan Earrings

Choose your favorite color of paper for these great earrings. Double-sided metallic or other origami paper works best. You can also try other decorative papers or magazine paper.

You will need:

- a square of double-sided origami paper, 15 cm x 15 cm (6 in. x 6 in.)
- 2 strips of contrasting paper, 0.5 cm x 15 cm (¼ in. x 6 in.)
- varnish or Podge and brush (optional)
- 2 jewelry rings, 0.75 cm (⅜ in.) diameter
- 2 earring hooks
- scissors, glue stick, paper clips, cutting board, small nail, hammer, pair of pliers

1 Cut the origami square in half. Put one half aside.

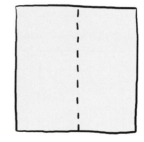

2 Fold over a 0.5 cm (¼ in.) strip on the short end of the paper. Turn the paper over and fold again in the other direction. Continue turning and folding until you reach the top.

3 Fold the folded strip in half. Open and spread glue along the outside of the last folded section. Fold in half again and press the glued sides together. Hold together with paper clips until dry.

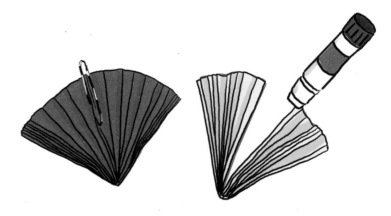

4 Spread glue along one side of a strip of contrasting paper. Wind the strip around the folded fan about 0.5 cm (¼ in.) from the folded top. Let dry.

5 Make a hole to hang your fan by having an adult help you hammer a nail through all the layers of paper.

6 Open a jewelry ring with a pair of pliers. Thread the ring into the hole, add an earring hook and close the ring with the pliers.

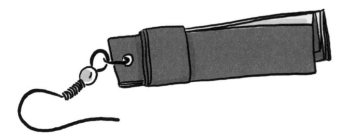

7 Spread your fan into an open position. Paint varnish on it to help it hold its shape and make it glossy, if you like. Let dry.

8 Repeat to make the second earring, using the other half of paper you put aside in step 1.

◤ Other Ideas:

● Make a gift card. Fold a piece of heavy art paper or card stock in half. Glue the fan to the front. Hold it in place firmly by sewing it on, using metallic or decorative thread.

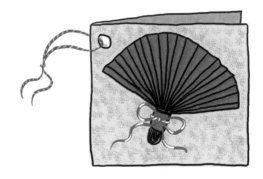

● Use fans to make a mobile (page 15) or to decorate a wreath (page 140) or the top of a gift box (page 44).

Wise King Doll

This wise king is tucked into a traditional Japanese holder called a Noshi. Small gifts are wrapped in these to wish someone luck or congratulations.

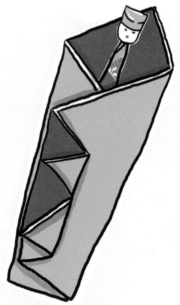

◣ You will need:

- a bamboo or thin wooden skewer (available at grocery stores)
- 2 strips of white paper, 1 cm x 27 cm (½ in. x 11 in.)
- a piece of gold paper, 1 cm x 4 cm (½ in. x 1½ in.)
- a square of wrapping or origami paper, 8 cm x 8 cm (3 in. x 3 in.)
- 2 squares of contrasting wrapping or origami paper, 15 cm x 15 cm (6 in. x 6 in.)
- glue stick, thin black marker or pen, pencil, ruler

1 Break the skewer to 8 cm (3 in.) long.

2 Spread glue along one side of a strip of white paper. Lay the skewer on one end. Tightly wind the paper around. Repeat, winding the second strip over the first.

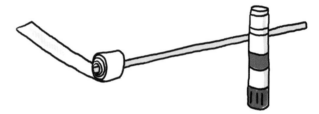

3 Spread glue along one long side of the gold paper. Wrap it around the top of the white paper. Spread glue on the overlapping edge and press together. Let dry.

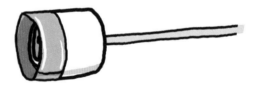

4 Squeeze the sides of the gold paper to make a crown.

5 Spread glue along one edge of the wrapping paper. Lay the skewer down on an angle and curl the glued side of the paper over it. Fold to the middle of the paper, making a triangular shape.

6 Fold the other side of the paper over and glue down. Draw a face and hair on the head of the doll.

7 To make the Noshi, place the contrasting papers back to back, colored sides out. Mark 5 cm (2 in.) sections along the top. Mark 2.5 cm (1 in.) from the bottom left corner along the side. Score (page 8) and fold, connecting the marks as shown.

8 Fold up about 7 cm (2¾ in.) of the bottom section.

9 Fold the right side over the folded sections.

10 Fold the corner back to the right, making the fold match the side edge. Fold the corner back to the left to complete the zigzag pattern. Secure the holder with glue behind the folds. Put the king doll inside.

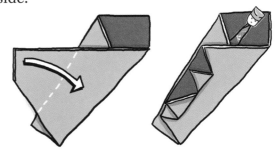

◼ **Other Ideas:**

Make a Noshi cup with red and pink papers for Valentine's Day. Fill it with cinnamon heart candies for a unique gift.

Card Box

This is a great way to use an old greeting card. Quick and easy, this beautiful box is perfect for jewelry or a special little gift.

You will need:

- an old greeting card
- scissors, pencil, ruler, glue stick, paper clips

1 Cut the card in half along the fold.

2 Put the front of the card face down and measure a 2.5 cm (1 in.) margin around all four sides. Score (page 8).

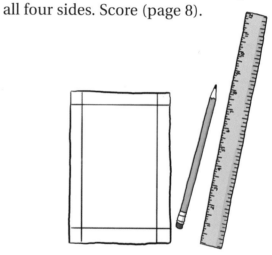

3 Fold along all the scored lines. Open.

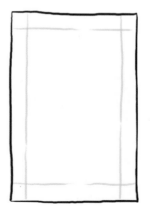

4 Cut along the fold lines of the short sides from the outer edge to the inside fold lines, as shown.

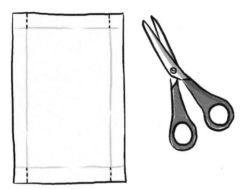

5 Fold up the sides.

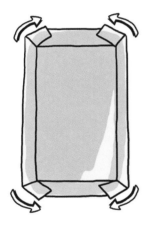

6 Put glue on the back of the short folded flaps. Press these to the side flaps. Hold in place with paper clips until dry.

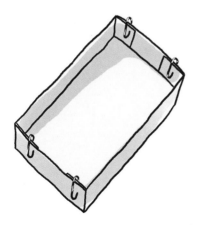

7 Cut off a 0.5 cm (¼ in.) strip on the long side of the back of the card.

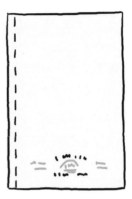

8 Repeat steps 2 to 6 with the back to make the bottom of your box.

◣ Other Ideas:

Vary the size and depth of your box by altering the size of the margin and using different sizes of cards.

Wrapping Paper Box

You can use any wrapping, decorative or plain paper to make this sturdy box. It is perfect for holding school photos, beads or small mementos from a trip.

◨ You will need:

- a square of wrapping paper, 24 cm x 24 cm (9½ in. x 9½ in.)

- a square of wrapping paper, 23 cm x 23 cm (9 in. x 9 in.)

- scissors

1 Fold one square in half diagonally. Open it. Repeat with the other diagonal. Open.

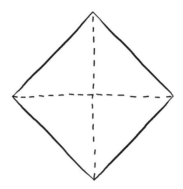

2 Fold a corner in to the center. Open it. Repeat with all corners.

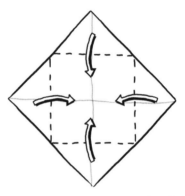

3 Fold a corner up to meet the fold line above the center fold. Open it. Fold the same corner to meet the closest fold line. Open. Repeat with all corners.

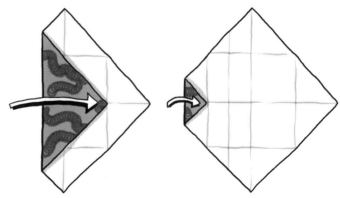

4 With a corner pointing flat toward you, cut along two fold lines on either side of the center fold. Make your cut only two folds long — don't cut as far as the center line. Repeat on the opposite side.

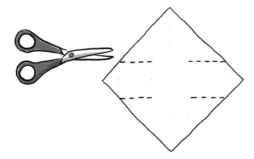

5 Fold the top and bottom corners in so that the points touch the center. Fold the top and bottom sides in to meet at the center. Sharpen the folds (page 8).

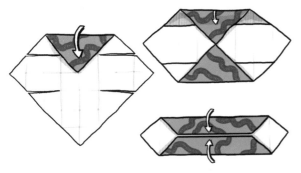

6 Open the top and bottom sides to stand up. Fold the cut pieces of the top and bottom sides in to meet at the middle. Sharpen these folds.

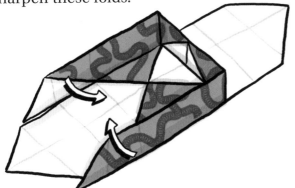

7 Lift the remaining top and bottom sections over and in to the middle, pressing the corners flat into the bottom of the box. Sharpen all folds.

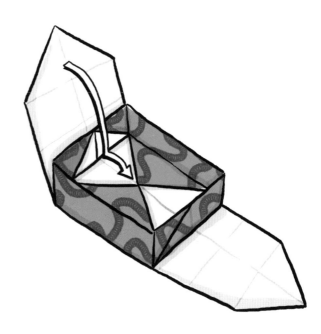

8 Repeat with the other square to make the bottom of your box.

◼ Other Ideas:

• Make any size of box. Just make sure that one square is 1 cm (½ in.) smaller than the other.

• Glue or sew a kimono (page 36), fan (page 38) or pom-pom (page 83) on top.

Gift Bag

Decorate your paper with stencil patterns or stamping to make a really special gift bag.

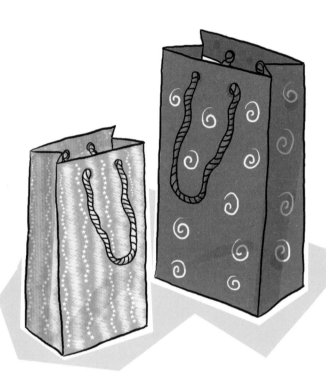

You will need:

- a piece of art paper or wallpaper, 30 cm x 56 cm (12 in. x 22½ in.)
- a piece of thin cardboard, 8.5 cm x 17.25 cm (3¼ in. x 6⅞ in.)
- 2 pieces of decorative cord, 15 cm (6 in.) long
- ruler, pencil, glue stick, hole punch

1 Score (page 8) and fold over a 2.5 cm (1 in.) flap along the top of the paper.

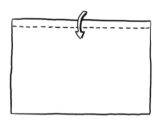

2 Fold a 2 cm (¾ in.) flap along one side of the paper. Fold another flap 6 cm (3 in.) from the bottom.

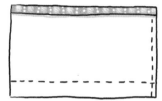

3 Fold the paper in half, keeping the side, top and bottom flaps folded. Open it.

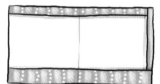

4 Fold over 9 cm (3¾ in.) from the left side. Open it. Fold over 18 cm (7 in.) from the right side. Open it. Lightly label the sections as shown.

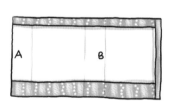

5 Fold section B in half lengthwise, creating a mountain fold (page 8) in the middle. Repeat with section A.

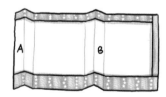

6 Open the bottom flap. Fold the right corner up to the fold line.

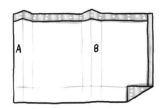

7 Open the corner and the side flap. Reverse the side flap fold in the bottom flap, creating a mountain fold. Bring this mountain fold in to meet the valley fold of the bottom flap. The side fold will stand up.

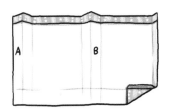

8 Stand the bottom section up. Push the right side fold of section A down to the right, meeting the base and lifting the sides as you do. Sharpen the fold and open it.

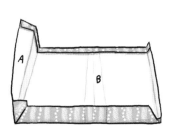

9 Repeat step 8 with the left side of section B, folding it to the left.

10 Repeat step 8 with the right side of section B, folding it to the right.

11 Spread glue along the outside of the side flap. Tuck the bottom of the side flap into the base of section A. Slip the top under the fold. Press the side down and leave to dry.

12 Turn the bag upright and press the bottom sections flat. Glue them in place. Put the cardboard in the bottom of the bag to give it extra strength.

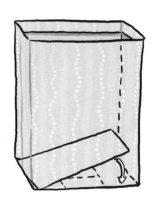

13 Punch two holes at the top of each middle section. Pull the cord through from the inside and knot it at both ends.

Never-ending Ornament

This ornament can also be a small book where you can write a never-ending story.

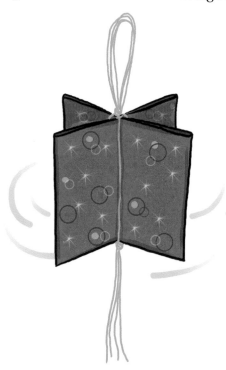

You will need:

- a piece of bond or art paper, 35 cm x 10 cm (14 in. x 4 in.)
- 2 pieces of metallic or embroidery thread, 70 cm (28 in.) long
- glue stick
- a pen or marker (optional)

1 Fold over a 1 cm (½ in.) flap at one end of the paper.

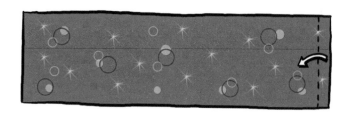

2 Fold the paper in half widthwise. Open it. Bring each end in to meet at the fold. Sharpen the folds (page 8).

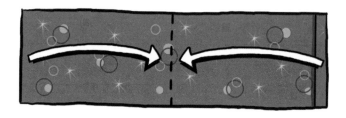

3 Bring the folded edges in to meet at the center. Sharpen the folds. Open.

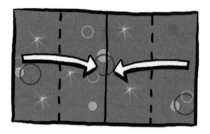

4 Beginning with the flap end, re-fold all folds so that they alternate between valley and mountain folds (page 8). Sharpen all folds.

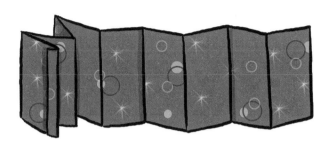

5 Spread glue along the front side of the flap. Press the back side of the other end of the paper on top of this flap, matching the end with the fold. Let dry.

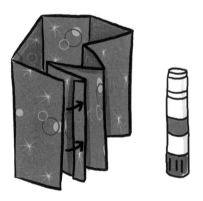

6 Holding the threads together, fold them in half. Make a knot 8 cm (3 in.) from the folded end.

7 Pinch all the valley folds together. Place a strand of thread in each valley fold. Grab all four threads at the bottom of the paper and pull taut. Knot together.

8 Open each section. If you like, write a story or draw on each "page" to make a book with no beginning and no ending.

◤ Other Ideas:

Hang your ornament from a mobile (page 15) or give it as a special gift in a box (pages 42–45).

Japanese Doll Bookmark

If you use patterned origami paper, your doll will look as if she is wearing a kimono.

◥ You will need:

- 1 square of origami paper, 15 cm x 15 cm (6 in. x 6 in.), cut in half
- a strip of thin cardboard, 2.5 cm x 10.5 cm (1 in. x 4¼ in.)
- a piece of contrasting paper, 1 cm x 9 cm (½ in. x 3½ in.)
- a piece of white bond paper, 22 cm x 27 cm (8½ in. x 11 in.)
- a piece of black paper, cut into a half circle about 4 cm (1½ in.) in diameter
- glue stick, scissors, toothpick, marker

1 Place the cut origami papers on top of each other, back to back.

2 Fold over a 1 cm (½ in.) strip along the top edge. Turn the papers over.

3 Fold the papers in half lengthwise. Open. Fold the left corner at a slight angle so that the point crosses over the middle fold. Fold the right corner to cross over the middle, slightly overlapping the left corner.

4 Spread glue on the strip of cardboard. Place the cardboard so that the top rests under the folded corners. Let dry.

5 Fold the right side over the cardboard. Fold back the bottom corner.

6 Fold the second side to overlap the first. Fold back the bottom corner.

7 Spread glue along the piece of contrasting paper. Place the center of the paper on the middle of the kimono, about 4 cm (1½ in.) from the top point. Fold it around to the back of the kimono and overlap the ends. Press it down to hold the kimono in place. Let dry.

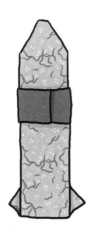

8 To make the doll's head, cut two ovals, about 2.5 cm (1 in.) long, out of the white paper.

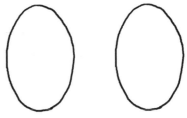

9 Spread glue on one of the ovals. Place the toothpick in the center and cover with the second oval. Let dry.

10 Glue the black paper to the back of the doll's head.

11 Draw a face on your doll. Put a bit of glue on the toothpick and push it down into the middle of the kimono.

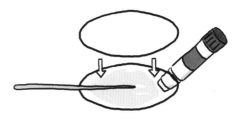

Decorative Envelope

Use this envelope when you want to give someone a gift certificate, or fill it with confetti hearts for a special valentine.

◆ You will need:

- a square of heavy art paper or wrapping paper, 30 cm x 30 cm (12 in. x 12 in.)
- a circle of contrasting art paper, approximately 2.5 cm (1 in.) in diameter
- ruler, pencil, scissors, hole punch, decorative-edge scissors (optional), brass paper fastener
- ribbon, 0.25 cm (⅛ in.) wide

1 Measure 8 cm (3 in.) margins on two opposite sides of the paper square and 10 cm (4 in.) margins on the other sides.

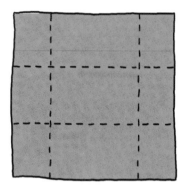

2 Draw curved flaps as shown, going from the middle rectangle out to the top mid-point of each side. Cut along the curves.

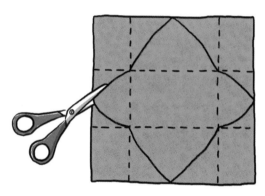

3 Score along the lines (page 8). Fold the sides in, then the top and bottom.

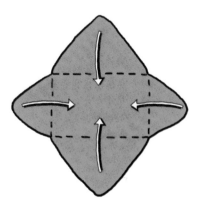

4 Mark a point in the middle of the top flap. Punch a small hole.

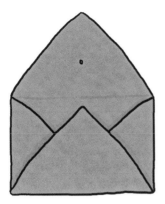

5 Use decorative-edge scissors, if you have them, to trim around the edge of the paper circle. Punch a hole in the center.

6 Match the hole in the circle with the hole in your envelope. Put a paper fastener through both holes and open it at the back.

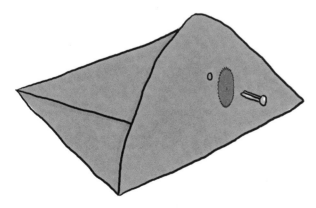

7 Wind the middle of the ribbon between the circle and the envelope. Tie the ribbon around the envelope, winding over the top and bottom, then around the sides. Tie the ribbon ends around the circle.

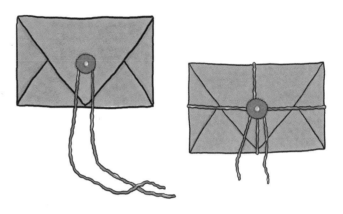

◤ Other Ideas:

Experiment with different sizes of paper and different margins to make a variety of shapes. Use fabric ribbon and different decorative-edge scissors to make unique designs.

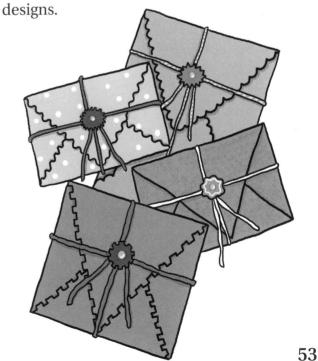

See-through Envelope

Put pressed flowers or shiny confetti between layers of tracing or wax paper to make this unusual envelope.

■ You will need:

- 2 squares of tracing or wax paper, at least 18 cm x 18 cm (7 in. x 7 in.)
- a plate, about 15 cm (6 in.) in diameter
- small dried flowers or petals, small photos or shiny confetti
- pencil, scissors, glue stick

1 Draw a circle on each piece of paper by tracing around the plate. Cut the circles out.

2 Place dried flowers, photos or confetti face down on one circle. Put dots of glue on the back of the objects and around the outside of the circle. Press the other circle on top.

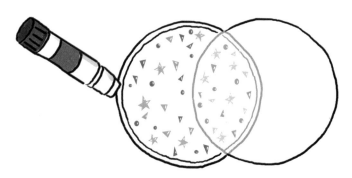

3 Fold over about a third of the side of the circles, as shown.

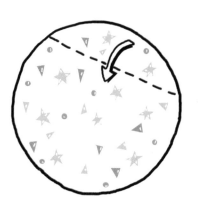

4 Fold over the other side, overlapping the lower section of the first fold.

5 Fold over the last side, folding at the corners and overlapping the other sides, making a triangle. Sharpen all folds (page 8).

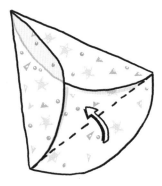

6 Open the one side. Slide your card in. Tuck the side of the last flap under the fold beside it.

 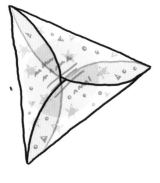

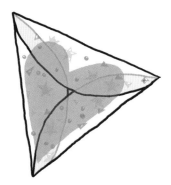

Other Ideas:

• This envelope works well for a small card about 7 cm (2¾ in.) in diameter. See page 152 for a handmade paper medallion that fits perfectly.

• Use different kinds of paper and different sizes of plates for other envelopes. Use one layer for non-see-through envelopes. Or combine layers of see-through and non-see-through paper.

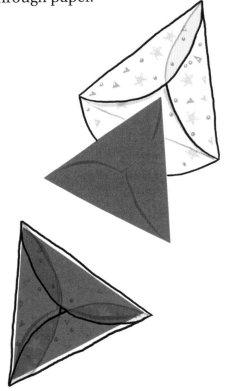

Paper Cutting

Have you ever made snowflake patterns by folding and cutting paper? There are many more unique and unusual patterns that you can make using different combinations of cuts, folds and piercings. Paper-cutting techniques have been used by people all over the world for more than 1000 years. Your paper-cut pieces can be used for signs, decorations, cards, bookmarks, picture frames, even for puppets! Here is a variety of paper-cutting projects — and ideas for lots more.

TIPS:

◤ Try using decorative-edge scissors instead of regular scissors for your crafts. They come in lots of fun shapes.

◤ Sometimes you need to cut more accurately than is possible with scissors. Some crafts suggest using an X-Acto or craft knife. Remember to use a cutting board, and always ask an adult for help when you use a knife.

StarLight
Star Bright
First Star
I see tonight

ARTY

Glow Lamp

This cut-paper decoration wraps around a glass jar. When a candle is lit in the jar, you get a warm, glowing stained-glass effect.

◤ You will need:

- a piece of black construction paper
- small pieces of tissue paper in many different colors
- a small glass jar, such as a jam jar
- a small candle, such as a tea light
- scissors, white glue and small glue brush or glue stick, newspaper, paper clips

1 Cut the construction paper in half lengthwise. Bend one of the pieces into a circle that fits over the jar without touching it. Make sure that it is long enough to overlap by 1 cm (½ in.). Glue on some extra construction paper if you need to make the circle larger.

2 Fold the paper in half three times. Press down the folds.

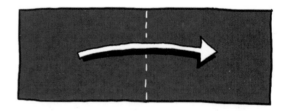

58

3 Cut out simple shapes along the fold lines. Heart, wedge or scallop shapes work well. Do not cut at the bottom of the folds. Open the paper.

4 Put the paper on newspaper and spread a small amount of glue around the edge of one of the shapes. Try not to get glue on the newspaper. Place a piece of tissue paper over the glue. Press down and trim off excess, if necessary.

5 Continue until you have covered all the shapes. You may need to use a clean sheet of newspaper after a few shapes to avoid getting glue on the front of the construction paper.

6 Glue the ends together on the inside to make a circle. Hold together with paper clips until dry.

7 Put a candle in the jar and ask an adult to help you light it. Place the paper shade over the jar.

Valentine's Hearts

These cutout hearts can be used for a window decoration, a card, or to create an unusual frame by putting photographs behind them.

You will need:

- a piece of red construction paper
- scissors, pencil, X-Acto or craft knife, cutting board

1 Fold the paper in half. Fold it in half again in the other direction.

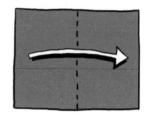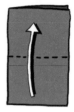

2 Cut out two half heart shapes, as shown.

3 Draw a full heart in the middle area and use an X-Acto knife to cut it out.

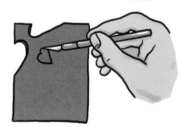

4 Cut a scalloped edge along the diagonal line, as shown. Open.

Other Ideas:

Make your paper cutting with white paper and glue a sheet of red tissue paper behind it.

60

Starry Night

This pattern makes a beautiful window decoration, sign or card.

You will need:

- a piece of dark blue construction or decorative paper
- a piece of light-colored paper or tissue paper
- a dinner plate
- pencil, scissors, X-Acto or craft knife, cutting board

1 Trace around the plate on the construction paper. Use regular or decorative-edge scissors to cut out the circle.

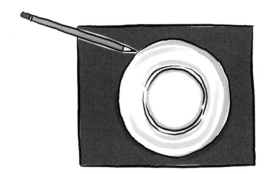

2 Fold the circle in half. Fold it in half again.

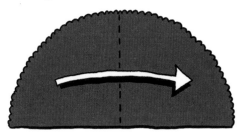

3 Draw star shapes, as shown, making several whole stars and half stars on the edge of the folds. Draw a quarter star at the point.

4 Use an X-Acto knife to cut out the stars. Open the circle. Glue it onto a sheet of colored paper or glue tissue paper to the back (page 59, steps 4 and 5) and hang your starry night in a window.

Name Silhouette

A name silhouette makes a unique design to use as a place card, gift label, picture frame or door sign.

You will need:

- a piece of construction or wrapping paper
- a piece of contrasting heavy art paper or card stock, the same size as the construction or wrapping paper
- crayon, pencil, scissors, glue stick, X-Acto or craft knife

1 Fold the construction paper in half widthwise, wrong side facing out. Using the crayon, write your name in script along the fold line. If you have descending letters in your name (for example "y" or "p"), write your name above the fold line, with the descending letters touching the fold.

2 Trace around the edges of the crayon line with a pencil. Your crayon lines should be about 0.5 cm (¼ in.) thick. Draw outside the lines if you need to make them fatter.

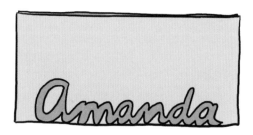

3 Cut out along the lines. Use an X-Acto knife to cut inside the letters. Do not cut where the letters touch the fold.

4 Open your name silhouette. Glue it to the contrasting paper.

NAME FRAME

This works only if you have a descending or ascending letter at the beginning or end of your name.

Use a folded piece of paper that is at least 15 cm (6 in.) long. Write your name so that the long letters touch the fold line. Cut out your name silhouette, leaving the fold uncut, and glue it onto contrasting paper.

Other Ideas:

Use your name on a more complicated folding pattern.

1. Fold a square of bond paper in half, then in half the other way.

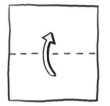

2. Fold it diagonally to make a triangle. Fold again if you wish.

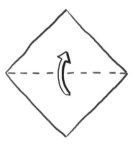

3. Write your name with a crayon, stretching the letters to touch each other and both sides of the paper.

4. Cut out, leaving the folded edges uncut. Cut out the enclosed parts of the letters using an X-Acto or craft knife. Open.

Stencil Pattern Bookmark

Stencil patterns are great for cut-paper crafts. This one is easy to trace, so you'll be able to make lots of these special bookmarks for your favorite bookworms.

◢ You will need:

- a piece of tracing paper,
  27 cm x 14 cm (8½ in. x 5½ in.)

- 2 pieces of heavy art paper or card stock,
  3 cm x 14 cm (1¼ in. x 5½ in.)

- scraps of colored tissue paper

- ribbon or yarn

- pencil, tape, X-Acto or craft knife, cutting board,
  white glue and small glue brush or glue stick,
  scissors, hole punch

1 Trace the stencil pattern shown at the top of the next page. Put the pattern upside down on the back of one of the pieces of paper. Tape lightly in place. Go over the lines with a pencil, pressing heavily to make an impression.

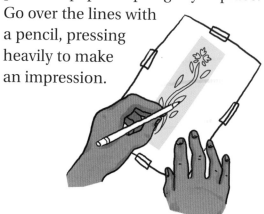

2 Use an X-Acto knife to cut out the pattern.

3 Dab glue carefully around the holes and glue tissue paper over them. Trim off any excess tissue.

stencil pattern

4 Spread glue around the edges of the paper, avoiding the tissue-paper holes. Glue the uncut paper to this piece. Let dry.

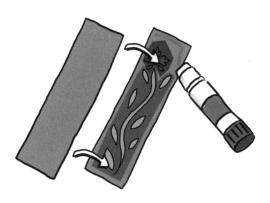

5 Punch a hole in the top and tie on the ribbon.

◣ Other Ideas:

Use stencil patterns to make cut-paper cards. Your library will have a pattern book.

1. Fold a paper circle or square 10 cm x 10 cm (4 in. x 4 in.) into eighths and draw on a stencil pattern. Cut it out with an X-Acto or craft knife.

2. Glue the finished cutout to a piece of folded heavy art paper or card stock, 18 cm x 25 cm (7 in. x 10 in.). The background color will shine through the holes.

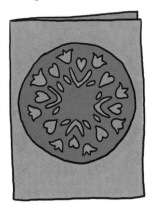

65

Kirigami

Kirigami is the Japanese art of paper cutting. The design shown here is a traditional cherry blossom pattern. You can use it as a design for your binder or a decoration for a card.

You will need:

- a square of decorative paper, such as origami foil paper, 15 cm x 15 cm (6 in. x 6 in.)
- a square of colored bond or art paper, 15 cm x 15 cm (6 in. x 6 in.)
- scraps of colored paper
- pencil, scissors, glue stick

1 Fold the square in half diagonally. Find the center of the diagonal and fold the right corner down from this mid-point. The corner should extend below the lower side, as shown.

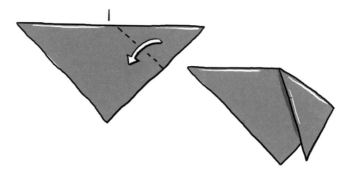

2 Fold the right side over to meet the folded edge.

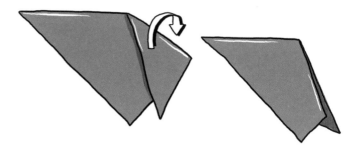

3 Fold the remaining left-hand point to the back so that it is even with the fold made in step 2.

4 Draw the shape as shown. The sections should be about 0.5 cm (¼ in.) wide.

5 Carefully cut out around the drawn shape. Open. Glue the cut design to a colored paper background.

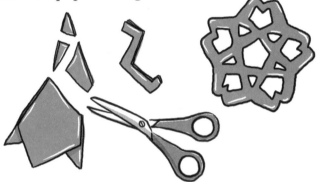

6 Cut colored paper to fit in the center and in the "petal" areas.

Other Ideas:

• Glue your Kirigami design to a piece of folded heavy art paper or card stock to make a card (page 65).

• You can also use a Kirigami design for decoupage (page 131). Put it on a small box for special treasures.

Orizomegami

Orizomegami is an easy paper-dyeing technique. Using paper towel and food coloring, you can make fabulous decorated paper for cards. Try different folds and color combinations to get other patterns.

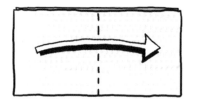 You will need:

- a sheet of paper towel
- food coloring in various colors
- a saucer for each color

1 Fold the paper towel in half, then in half again. Fold the towel diagonally to make a triangle.

2 Dip the folded sides into saucers of food coloring. You only need to touch the coloring briefly because the color will spread.

3 After you have dipped in two or three colors, open the paper towel. Let dry before attaching it to a card.

Cut-paper Cards

Simple geometric shapes cut out of heavy paper make great spaces to fill with Orizomegami.

◣ You will need:

- a piece of heavy art paper or card stock, 18 cm x 25 cm (7 in. x 10 in.)
- a piece of Orizomegami
- a piece of heavy art paper or card stock, 13 cm x 18 cm (5 in. x 7 in.)
- pencil, X-Acto or craft knife, cutting board, glue stick

1 Fold the large paper in half. Draw a window shape on the front.

2 Open the card and use an X-Acto knife to cut out the window shape.

3 Open the card to the inside. Put glue around the edge of the window and attach the Orizomegami or other decorated paper.

4 Spread glue on the left side of the card, around the Orizomegami. Glue the smaller piece of heavy paper on top.

◣ Other Ideas:

Orizomegami looks great behind any cut-paper design. Try it with the valentine's hearts (page 60), starry night (page 61) or stencil pattern bookmark (page 64).

Cookie Cutter Cards

This card combines an accordion fold with a cutout paper window. Use your favorite cookie cutter for a pattern.

Starlight
Star Bright
First Star
I See tonight

◤ You will need:

- a piece of heavy art paper or card stock, 22 cm x 35 cm (8½ in. x 14 in.)
- a cookie cutter, not more than 9 cm (3½ in.) wide
- 3 pieces of tissue paper in a contrasting color, 8 cm x 10 cm (3 in. x 4 in.) or large enough to cover the cookie cutter
- a piece of heavy art paper or card stock, 9 cm x 22 cm (3½ in. x 8½ in.)
- pencil, X-Acto or craft knife, cutting board, glue stick

1 Fold the long paper in half widthwise.

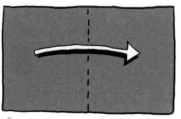

2 Fold one end to meet the center fold. Turn the paper over and repeat with the other end.

3 Put the cookie cutter on the front of your card. Make sure it doesn't touch the sides. Trace around the cookie cutter.

4 Open the card and use an X-Acto knife to cut out the shape.

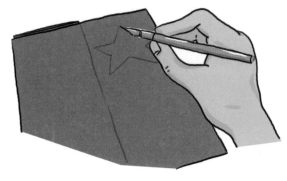

5 Close the card and trace around the shape.

6 Cut through all layers with an X-Acto knife. You may have to go over your cuts several times to get through all the paper.

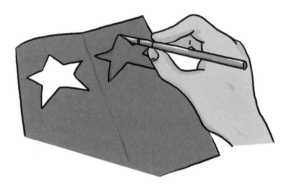

7 Glue one piece of tissue paper to the back of the last section, pushing it through the shape a little so that it is slightly puffy. Glue on the other two pieces in the same way. Trim any excess tissue paper.

8 Glue the smaller piece of heavy paper to the back of your card.

◼ Other Ideas:

● Use one cookie cutter pattern for the first two panels of your accordion fold and a different one for the second two. Cover the holes in the second and third panels the same way that you did in steps 7 and 8.

● For a stained-glass effect, cover the holes of the second, third and fourth panels with one piece of tissue paper each and leave off the backing (step 8).

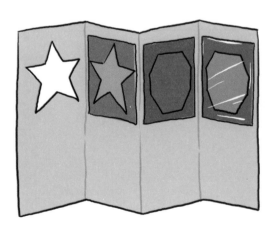

● Cover only the last hole with metallic, wrapping or Orizomegami paper (page 68) or fabric.

Pierced Paper Lace

You can make delicate writing paper or an interesting picture frame by piercing paper with a pin to make a lacy effect.

◤ You will need:

- a piece of white bond paper, 22 cm x 27 cm (8½ in. x 11 in.)
- a piece of colored bond paper, 22 cm x 27 cm (8½ in. x 11 in.)
- a piece of colored heavy art paper or card stock, 20 cm x 25 cm (8 in. x 10 in.), for the frame
- pencil, tape, stack of newspapers, large needle or push pin, scissors, X-Acto or craft knife

◤ WRITING PAPER

1 On the bond paper, draw a simple design.

2 Lightly tape the design to the top of the colored bond paper. Place the paper on the newspapers.

3 Starting on one design line, press the needle through both layers of paper. Continue along the line, making the holes evenly spaced and close together. Keep at least the width of a hole separating the holes.

4 To increase the size of the holes and make a more distinct design, wiggle the needle as you make each hole. You can also vary the size of the holes for different parts of the design.

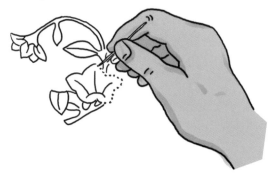

5 When finished, gently remove the cover paper.

6 Trim the edge of the paper to match the edge of your design, leaving at least a 1 cm (½ in.) margin.

▧ PIERCED PAPER FRAME

1 Draw a 6 cm (2¼ in.) margin around the heavy art paper.

2 Repeat steps 1 to 5 for the writing paper.

3 Use an X-Acto knife to trim around the rectangle, following the line of the lace pattern. Do not cut the outside edge of the frame.

4 Tape a 10 cm x 15 cm (4 in. x 6 in.) photograph or picture to the back of the frame.

▧ Other Ideas:

● Pierced paper can be used to make special placemats, cards or window displays.

● Use stencil patterns for your designs, piercing around the edge of the stencil.

● Make a small paper cylinder with pierced paper and fit it around a glass jar with a candle in it. See the glow lamp (page 58).

Shadow Puppets

Shadow puppets originally come from Indonesia, where they are made from thin leather. The puppets are used in front of a white sheet, screen or wall. When a light shines on them, they cast shadows on the screen. Moving parts and punched holes give them extra details. Once you've made this frog and prince, invent other characters and stage a whole play.

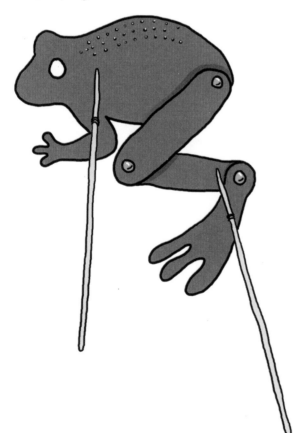

You will need:

- a piece of heavy art paper or card stock
- 5 wooden skewers (available at grocery stores)
- pencil, scissors, stack of newspapers, large needle or push pin, hole punch, brass paper fasteners, needle and strong thread

FROG

1 Draw the body of a frog, as shown, on heavy paper. Draw the three leg pieces separately. Make the ends of the leg pieces at least 1.5 cm (½ in.) wide. Cut out all the pieces.

2 Cut out the eye. Put the frog body on the newspapers and poke holes with the needle to make the back details.

3 Place the large leg piece on the body as shown. Punch a hole through both layers and fasten with a paper fastener.

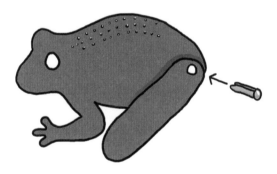

4 Attach the second leg piece to the first, make a hole and fasten with a paper fastener. Repeat with the third leg piece.

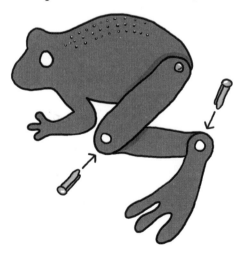

5 Place the end of a skewer on the body, just above the front leg. Push a threaded needle from the back of the paper to the front, cross over the skewer and sew into the back. Gently pull tight and go through the same holes again. Tighten and knot at the back. Trim off excess thread.

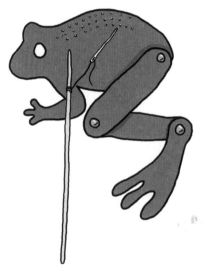

6 Repeat step 5 on the third leg piece.

7 Put a drop of white glue on the thread where it crosses over the skewers. Let dry.

◤ PRINCE

1 Draw and cut out the body and arms as shown. Enlarge the pieces, if you like.

2 Put the prince on the newspapers and poke holes for decorations and details as shown (see step 2 of the frog).

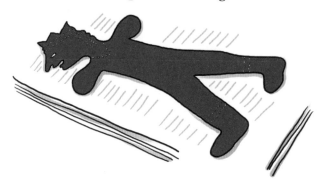

3 Attach the arms with paper fasteners (see steps 3 and 4 of the frog).

4 Attach one skewer to the body and one to each hand (see steps 5 and 7 of the frog).

◾ USING YOUR PUPPETS

Set up a light that you can shine at a blank wall or sheet hung on the wall. Turn out all the other lights and hold up your puppet, keeping yourself out of the light as much as possible. Experiment with the distance at which you hold the puppet from the wall. The shadow will change size depending on the puppet's distance from the wall. The moving parts will make your puppet very expressive.

77

Stained-Glass Window

You can use any stencil pattern to make a beautiful tissue-paper "stained-glass" window. This pattern is based on a real stained-glass window made more than 100 years ago.

You will need:

- a piece of white bond paper, 22 cm x 27 cm (8½ in. x 11 in.)
- a piece of black construction or heavy art paper
- scraps of tissue paper in a variety of bright colors
- scissors or X-Acto or craft knife, tape, white glue and glue brush or glue stick

1 Use a photocopier to enlarge the pattern shown here to the size you want for your window.

2 Tape the pattern to the black paper. Cut out the shapes using the X-Acto knife, cutting through both papers.

3 Remove the white pattern paper.

4 Dab glue on the back of the black paper, around the edge of the shape. Lay a piece of tissue over the shape and press in place.

5 Carefully trim any excess tissue paper.

6 Continue until you have filled in the whole picture with tissue paper. Let dry. Tape to a window to let the light shine through.

Other Ideas:

Borrow a book of stained-glass or stencil patterns from the library. Or design your own. The trick to designing your own window is to make a pattern by drawing the shapes between the lines, not the lines themselves.

Crepe-Paper Rose

Make lots of these elegant flowers and tie them into a bunch with a matching ribbon.

◣ You will need:

- red crepe-paper streamer (or another color suitable for roses)
- green crepe-paper streamer
- a piece of thin wire, 30 cm (12 in.) long
- 3 pieces of thin wire, 20 cm (8 in.) long
- scissors, glue stick, pencil, thread

1 Cut two pieces of red crepe paper, each 25.5 cm (10 in.) long. Gently dot glue along one and press them together. Let dry.

2 Fold the crepe paper in half three times. Draw a petal shape on the paper. Cut it out. Don't cut across the sides of the bottom section.

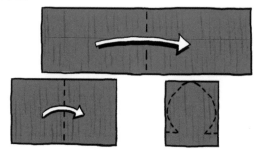

3 Open the paper into a chain of petals. Press the center of each petal with your thumbs and stretch the crepe paper.

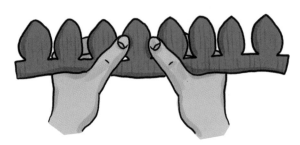

4 Fold over 2.5 cm (1 in.) at one end of the long wire. Begin to curl the petal chain around the wire, tightly rolling the first two petals. Continue to wind the petals around, less tightly, pleating the bottom edge as you go. Finish by tying thread tightly around the base.

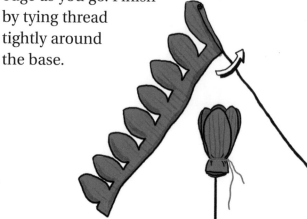

5 Cut an 8 cm (3 in.) piece of green crepe paper. Cut out peaked shapes as shown. Leave a 1 cm (½ in.) margin along the bottom.

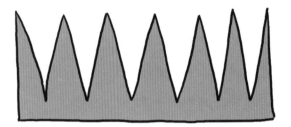

6 Spread glue along the bottom margin and wind tightly around the base of the petals.

7 Cut a 15 cm (6 in.) piece of green crepe paper. Fold in half. Cut out three pairs of leaf shapes.

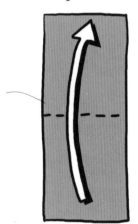
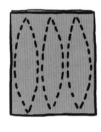

8 Lay a piece of wire on a leaf. Dab glue on a second leaf. Press the leaves together with the wire in the middle. Let dry while you repeat to make two more leaves. Twist all three wires together.

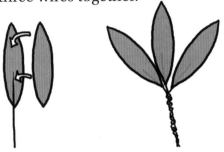

9 Cut a 60 cm (24 in.) piece of green crepe paper in half lengthwise. Put glue on one end. Wind this around the base of your flower three times.

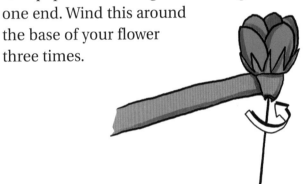

10 Continue winding down the wire. Add the leaf wires about 4 cm (1½ in.) from the top and wrap the green crepe paper over all four wires. Continue to the bottom and secure with glue. Open and spread the leaves.

Tissue Flowers

Try different color combinations for bright bouquets of these easy tissue-paper flowers.

You will need:

- 3 pieces of tissue paper in contrasting colors
- green floral tape or green crepe-paper streamer, 75 cm (30 in.) long and cut to 1 cm (½ in.) wide
- a round saucer, about 10 cm (4 in.) in diameter
- thin wire, 23 cm (9 in.) long
- pencil, scissors, thread, glue stick

PETAL FLOWER

1 Lay two pieces of tissue paper on top of each other. Use the saucer to trace a circle onto the tissue. Cut out both layers.

2 Fold the circles in half, keeping them on top of each other. Fold in half again. Pinch the corner and curl one side in to the middle.

3 Wind thread around the bottom several times, tie tightly and cut. Gently pull the petals apart.

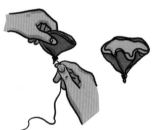

4 Make a small ball about 1 cm (½ in.) in diameter with the other piece of tissue paper. Glue it in the center of the petals.

5 Hook the wire into the thread at the bottom of the flower.

6 Glue and wind the floral tape or crepe paper tightly around the base and stem of the flower (page 81, steps 9 and 10).

POM-POM FLOWER

1 Cut three pieces of tissue paper 19 cm x 24 cm (7½ in. x 9½ in.). Place them on top of each other and fold in half lengthwise. Repeat twice more.

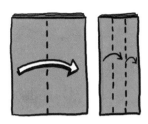

2 Fold the papers in half widthwise. Repeat. Open the last fold.

3 Cut a fringe from each end to the middle fold, leaving a 0.5 cm (¼ in.) margin in the center.

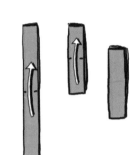

4 Fold in the middle. Fold the sides together.

5 Tightly wind thread about 0.5 cm (¼ in.) from the bottom. Knot and cut.

6 Trim the fringe, cutting off all the folds. Fluff out the pom-pom.

7 See steps 5 and 6 of the petal flower to add a stem.

◥ Other Ideas:

Use Orizomegami paper (page 68) instead of tissue paper for your flowers. You can use tiny pom-poms for barrettes (page 144), a mobile (page 15) or a gift card (page 94).

Silhouette Portrait

A silhouette is an old-fashioned way of making a portrait. You need two people to make a silhouette, one to draw and one to model. It's best to do it in a dark room.

◥ You will need:

- a piece of white paper or newsprint, 45 cm x 60 cm (18 in. x 24 in.)
- a bright lamp that you can aim
- a piece of black art paper, 45 cm x 60 cm (18 in. x 24 in.)
- a piece of light-colored paper, 45 cm x 60 cm (18 in. x 24 in.)
- masking tape, pencil, white pencil, scissors, glue stick

1 Tape the large white paper to a wall.

2 Sit the model sideways on a stool, approximately 30 cm (12 in.) from the paper on the wall.

3 Shine the lamp at the person's head. Turn off all other lights. Adjust the lamp position until the shadow of the model's head is clear on the paper.

4 Trace carefully around the edge of the shadow on the paper.

6 Place the head shape on the black paper and use the white pencil to trace around it. Cut it out.

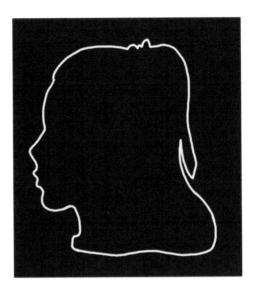

5 When you have traced all the way around the shadow, remove the paper from the wall and cut out the outline.

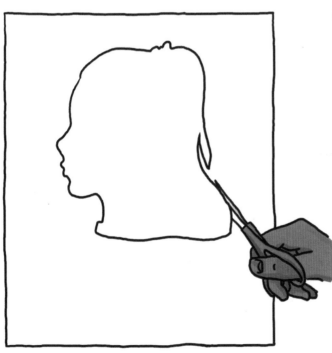

7 Glue the silhouette to the light-colored paper. Write the name of the person and the date on the back. Make a silhouette of the same person in five years — you'll be surprised at the difference!

Hanging Letter Banner

This is a perfect banner for any special occasion. Decorate each letter individually to make it really sparkle.

 You will need:

- a piece of black paper
- a piece of construction, wrapping or metallic paper for each letter, 12 cm x 30 cm (4½ in. x 12 in.)
- stickers, stamps, glitter glue, sparkles (optional)
- decorative cord or ribbon, about 2.5 m (8 ft.)
- white pencil, scissors, glue stick

1 Print your message in large block letters on the black paper. The letters shouldn't be larger than 9 cm x 9 cm (3½ in. x 3½ in.). Cut the letters out.

2 Fold each piece of construction paper in half, as shown.

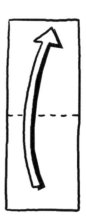

3 Glue each letter to the outside of a folded paper, keeping the fold at the top.

4 Decorate around the letters with stickers, stamps, glitter glue or sparkles.

5 Open the paper for the first letter of your greeting. Place the cord on the fold.

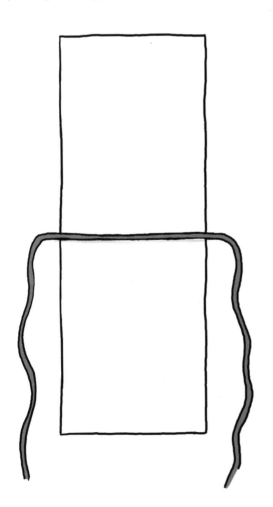

6 Glue along the back section of the paper, but leave a 2.5 cm (1 in.) space away from the fold and the cord. Fold the paper together and press.

7 Repeat with each letter along the length of the cord. Slide the letters to space them evenly and tie up the banner.

Picture Frame Book

This book is perfect for school photos. You can add additional frame pages when you have more pictures to include.

◤ You will need:

- 2 pieces of art paper, 13 cm x 24 cm (5 in. x 9½ in.)
- 2 pieces of contrasting art paper, 24 cm x 25 cm (9½ in. x 10 in.)
- 2 pieces of decorative cord or ribbon, 44 cm (17 in.) long
- glue stick, pencil, ruler, scissors, X-Acto or craft knife, cutting board, hole punch, 2 bulldog clips or clothespins
- a nail (optional)

1 Fold one of the smaller papers in half widthwise. Sharpen the fold (page 8). Open it. This will be the front cover.

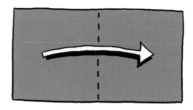

2 Spread glue inside one half of the cover. Press closed. Let dry under a heavy book. Repeat steps 1 and 2 with the second small paper to make a back cover.

3 Fold a piece of the contrasting paper in half widthwise. Sharpen the fold. Open it. Fold in half lengthwise, pressing to sharpen. Open it.

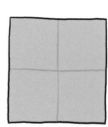

4 Mark a line 10.5 cm (4¼ in.) from each side on the top half of the paper. Cut out this rectangle from the center fold to the edge.

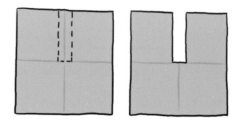

5 Draw margins 2.5 cm (1 in.) from the top, bottom and sides of the top sections. Use an X-Acto knife to cut the rectangles out of the center.

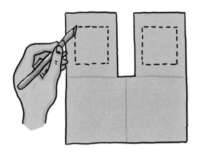

6 Fold the frame sections down, one in front and one behind the lower section. Fold the page in half. Sharpen the folds.

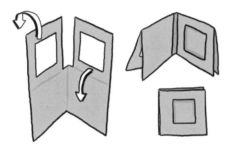

7 Repeat steps 3 to 6 with the second piece.

8 Punch two holes 1 cm (½ in.) from the back edge and 2.5 cm (1 in.) from the top and bottom of the folded page. Repeat with all pages and both covers.

9 Stack all four pages together, the covers on the top and bottom, the spine edges even. Hold in place with the bulldog clips.

10 Push one cord up through the top hole. Pull until half of it is through. Loop around the end of the book, then back through the same hole. Use a nail to help you push it through if you have trouble. Pull tight. Repeat with the other cord in the other hole.

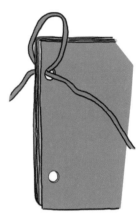

11 Tie each cord in a double knot, then tie them together. Glue photos to the paper behind the frames.

Paper Weaving

Crisscross and lace together different kinds of paper to make exciting and unusual patterns. Experiment with different combinations of paper widths, textures and colors to make your own designs for cards, bags, bookmarks or baskets.

A weaving grid is a series of crisscrossed lines that show your pattern.

Cut the lines of a grid in one direction only.

Always cut the paper strips a bit thinner than the weaving grid.

Combine thinner papers, like Japanese or wrapping paper, with heavy art papers.

Wallpaper makes great, strong woven patterns.

Cut the paper strips with decorative-edge scissors to make interesting edges.

Bookmark

This is a simple paper-weaving project. Add your own creative flair to it by choosing interesting contrasting paper.

◤ You will need:

- a strip of heavy art paper or card stock, 5 cm x 30 cm (2 in. x 12 in.)
- 3 strips of contrasting decorative paper, 0.75 cm x 15 cm (⅜ in. x 6 in.)
- ribbon, 20 cm (8 in.) long
- pencil, ruler, X-Acto or craft knife, cutting board, glue stick, wax paper, hole punch

1 Fold the strip of heavy paper in half widthwise. Open it. Mark a margin 0.5 cm (¼ in.) around the inside of one half of the paper.

2 Mark 1 cm (½ in.) sections around the rectangle. Connect the marks to make a crisscross pattern. This is your weaving grid (page 91).

3 Use the X-Acto knife to cut the short vertical lines in the paper. Do not cut through the first and last lines. Cut a slit in the center section of the vertical line next to the fold.

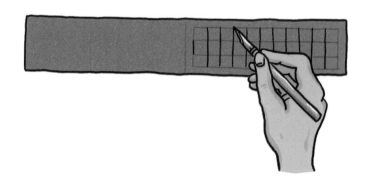

4 Beginning at the inside, by the fold, push a contrasting strip down through the first long cut line. Pull it through, leaving 0.75 cm (⅜ in.) at the end. Go up into the next cut line, pulling the strip to the inside. Push down through the next cut line, and so on, weaving until you reach the end.

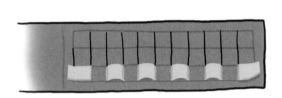

5 Repeat with the next strip, beginning at the short slit next to the fold. Weave this strip in the opposite sequence to the first one. Finish with the last strip, which should follow the woven pattern of the first strip.

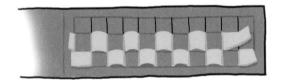

6 Gently pull all the strips tight and glue down the ends.

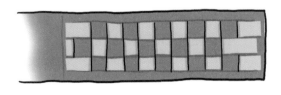

7 Spread glue on the unwoven half of the paper, fold it down and glue it to the back of your weaving. Put it between sheets of wax paper and place under a heavy book until dry.

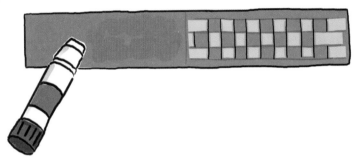

8 Punch a hole at the top (where there is less weaving) and attach a ribbon.

◤ Other Ideas:

Turn your woven bookmark into a napkin ring. Complete steps 1 to 7. After it is dry, overlap and glue the two ends. Hold together with paper clips or a clothespin until dry. Make a placemat to match (page 96).

Card

Use wrapping paper or other decorative paper for this card. It will look great with a woven gift bag to match (page 98).

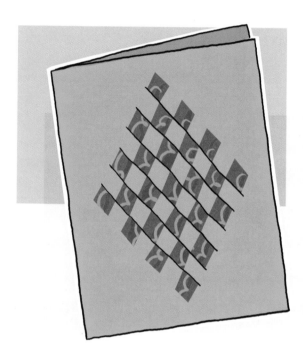

◤ You will need:

- a piece of heavy art paper or card stock, 16 cm x 25 cm (6½ in. x 10 in.)

- 9 strips of contrasting wrapping or decorative paper, (7 strips if you're using Imperial measurements) 0.75 cm x 14 cm (⅜ in. x 5½ in.)

- a piece of heavy art paper or card stock, 13 cm x 16 cm (5 in. x 6½ in.)

- pencil, ruler, X-Acto or craft knife, cutting board, glue stick

1 Fold the large paper in half widthwise. On the inside of one half, use a pencil and ruler to divide the paper into quarters. Draw a 1 cm (½ in.) margin around the outside.

2 Make a diamond by connecting the four points on the margin line.

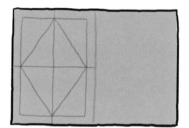

3 Make marks along each side of the diamond 1 cm (½ in.) apart. It's okay if the last section is a bit short. Connect the marks to make a weaving grid (page 91).

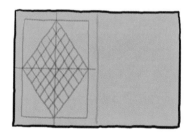

4 Use an X-Acto knife to cut one set of diagonal lines. Don't cut through the first and last lines.

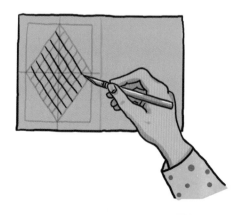

5 Cut slits along the first and last line, skipping every other section as shown.

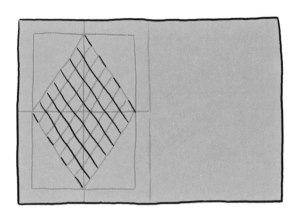

6 Push a contrasting strip down through the first slit. Pull it through, leaving 0.75 cm (⅜ in.) at the end. Go up through the first cut line, pulling the strip toward you. Push down through the next line, and so on, weaving until you reach the end.

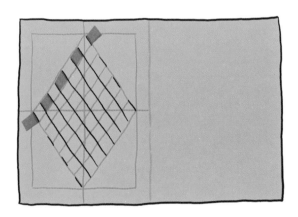

7 Repeat with a second strip, beginning at the first cut line. Weave this strip in the opposite sequence to the first one.

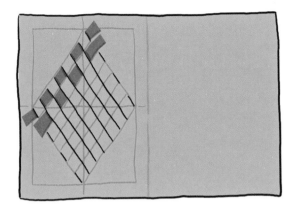

8 Repeat step 6 with a third strip. Continue to weave in all the strips.

9 Gently pull the strips tight, trim and glue down the ends.

10 Glue the smaller piece of heavy paper over the back of the weaving.

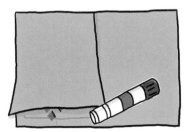

Placemat

Unusual papers and weaving patterns make this a very fancy table setting.

You will need:

- 2 pieces of heavy art paper or card stock, 30 cm x 40 cm (12 in. x 16 in.)
- a piece of contrasting decorative paper, 30 cm x 40 cm (12 in. x 16 in.)
- pencil, ruler, X-Acto or craft knife, cutting board, scissors, glue stick

1 Mark a 2.5 cm (1 in.) margin around all four sides of the wrong side of one piece of heavy paper.

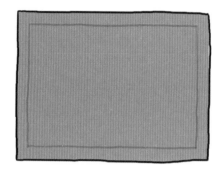

2 Draw either a diamond (page 94), a rectangle (page 92) or a diagonal (page 98) weaving grid on the heavy paper. Or draw curved lines horizontally or diagonally as shown. Make the lines different widths apart and use different kinds of curves.

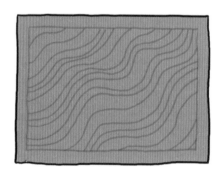

3 Cut the lines using an X-Acto knife (see steps 4 and 5, page 94).

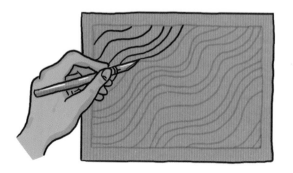

4 Cut strips of contrasting paper. If you want a regular pattern, and if your weaving grid uses 1 cm (½ in.) lines (page 94), cut the strips 0.75 cm (⅜ in.) wide. If you want an irregular pattern, experiment with different widths of strips.

5 Weave the strips (page 93) with the backs of your papers facing you. If you are using curved lines, don't worry if the strips do not always touch side by side. Weave each strip opposite from the one before it.

6 Pull the strips tight. Glue down the ends on the back of the mat. Glue on the second sheet of heavy paper as backing.

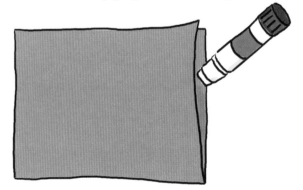

Other Ideas:

● Cover your placemat with clear adhesive vinyl (available at hardware stores) to protect it and make it waterproof.

● Make a napkin ring to match your placemat (page 93).

● Make a whole table setting of placemats and napkin rings for your family. Use the same color of heavy paper for all of them, but use different decorative papers so that every person has a unique place setting.

● Vary your weaving pattern by cutting some strips in half lengthwise. Alternate these with wider strips.

● Use a curved weaving pattern for a birthday card (page 94), making the paper strips with bright birthday wrapping paper.

97

Gift Bag

This project starts with a basic gift bag (page 46) and turns it into a present all on its own. Use metallic paper for a really special look. Make a woven card to match (page 94).

◤ You will need:

- a piece of art paper or wallpaper,
  30 cm x 56 cm (12 in. x 22 in.)

- 14 strips of contrasting wrapping,
  decorative or other paper,
  0.75 cm x 25 cm (⅜ in. x 10 in.)

- a piece of thin cardboard,
  8.5 cm x 17.25 cm (3½ in. x 6⅞ in.)

- 2 pieces of decorative cord, 15 cm (6 in.) long

- pencil, ruler, X-Acto or craft knife, cutting board,
  scissors, glue stick, hole punch

1 Use the art paper to make the gift bag on page 46, steps 1 to 10.

2 On the inside of the bag, draw a 2.5 cm (1 in.) margin around the edge of one of the large sections, as shown.

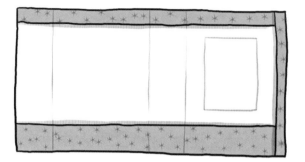

3 Make 1 cm (½ in.) marks around all sides of the rectangle. Draw lines connecting these marks diagonally, as shown.

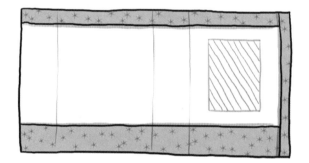

4 Use an X-Acto knife to cut along the diagonal lines.

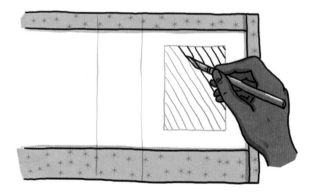

5 Beginning in the middle of the rectangle, push the first contrasting strip from the back to the front, through the first cut line. Continue to weave until you reach the end (page 95).

6 Begin the second strip beside the first, pushing through the second cut line. Weave through to the end. Begin another strip on the other side of the first, pushing through the second cut line and weaving in the same pattern as the second strip.

7 Begin the fourth strip beside the second, pushing through the third cut line. Weave to the end.

8 Continue in this way, weaving strips on opposite sides until the rectangle is completed.

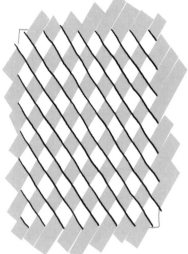

9 Trim off the excess from the strips. Gently pull the strips tight and glue the ends in place.

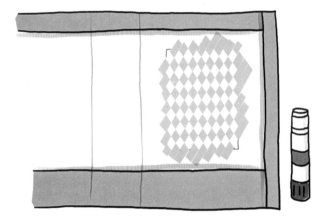

10 Repeat steps 2 to 8 on the other large section of the bag, if you like.

11 Finish your bag following steps 11 to 13 on page 47.

Basket

Turn a paper bag and wrapping paper into a gift basket or wastebasket. Make it seasonal by using holiday-patterned wrapping paper.

◤ You will need:

- 5 pieces of wrapping paper,
  3 cm x 53 cm (1¼ in. x 21 in.)

- 2 pieces of brown paper cut from a paper bag,
  15 cm x 30 cm (6 in. x 12 in.)

- 2 pieces of brown paper cut from a paper bag,
  7.5 cm x 38 cm (3 in. x 15 in.)

- white glue or glue stick, paper clips, pencil,
  ruler, scissors

1 Apply 1 cm (½ in.) of glue to one end of the wrong side of a piece of wrapping paper. Overlap this end with the other end, making a circle. Hold the circle in place with a paper clip until dry. Repeat with each piece of wrapping paper.

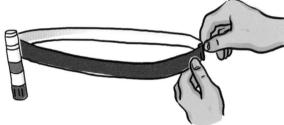

2 Mark an 8 cm (3 in.) section at one end of each wide piece of brown paper.

3 Spread glue on one of these sections. Place the marked section of the other wide piece over top, making one piece 53 cm (21 in.) long.

4 Spread glue on the center marked section of the glued papers. Put a narrow piece of paper on this area, matching the edge and attaching it at a right angle, as shown.

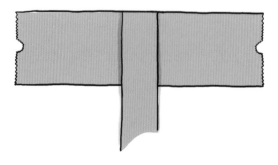

5 Turn the glued papers over. Repeat step 4 with the last piece of paper. The central glued area is the base for your basket.

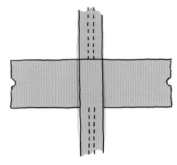

6 On each narrow side section, mark two lines approximately 3 cm (1¼ in.) from the side edges. Cut along these lines to the base.

7 On the wider sections, mark four lines approximately 3 cm (1¼ in.) apart. Cut along these lines to the base.

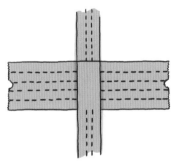

8 Hold a circle of wrapping paper over the base. Begin weaving by bringing one brown paper strip over the wrapping paper. Pull the next strip behind, the next over, the next behind, working around the circle. Attach the circle to the corners with paper clips.

9 Add a second circle beginning in the same place but pulling the strip behind the circle. Bring the next strip in front of the circle. Continue around, pulling the strips tight and holding them in place with paper clips, if necessary. Repeat this pattern with all the circles.

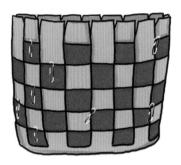

10 Trim the strips to 3 cm (1¼ in.). Fold each strip over, either in front or behind, depending on the pattern, and glue in place. Remove the paper clips.

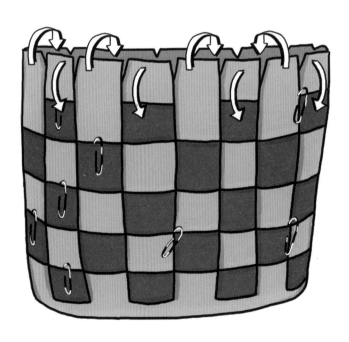

Valentine's Basket

Fill this little basket with cinnamon hearts for the perfect gift.

You will need:

- 1 piece of construction or heavy art paper, 12 cm x 30 cm (4¾ in. x 12 in.)
- 1 piece of contrasting construction or heavy art paper, 10 cm x 30 cm (4 in. x 12 in.)
- 2 ribbons, 20 cm (8 in.) long
- scissors, pencil, ruler, hole punch

1 Fold both pieces of paper in half widthwise. Cut off the corners of the open ends to round the tops.

2 Cutting from the folded side, make four slits in each paper, 12 cm (4½ in.) long. Vary the width of the sections to make an irregular pattern to your weave, if you like.

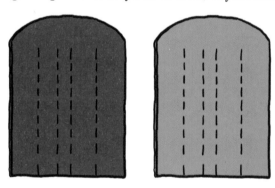

3 Holding the two pieces side by side, put the first section of side A inside the first section of side B.

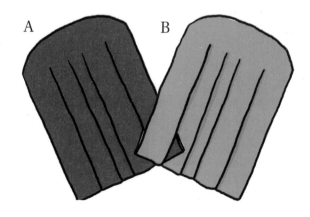

A   B

4 Put the first section of B into the next section of A. You may have to bend the paper a bit to do this.

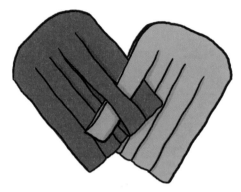

5 Put the third section of A into the first section of B, then B inside A, then A inside B. Pull the papers up to the ends of the slits.

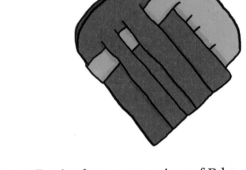

6 Begin the next section of B by placing it inside the first strip of A. Continue weaving the strips, alternating between inside and out, until you have finished all strips.

7 Open your basket and fold it along the opposite sides.

8 Punch holes through both papers at each side. Tie ribbon handles through the holes.

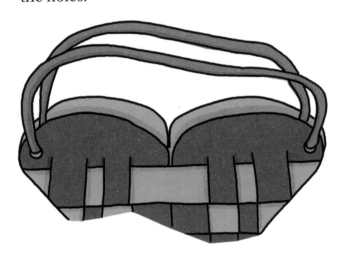

◢ Other Ideas:

You can easily change the size of this basket. To make one from larger paper, cut more slits in the papers. For a smaller one, make only two slits. Cut the slits a little longer than the width of your paper. Scraps of wallpaper make sturdy and decorative baskets.

Japanese Message Holder

This intriguing woven-paper project can be used as a message holder or a special card. Write your message on a separate piece of paper and tuck it into one of the folded pockets.

 You will need:

- 2 pieces of art or wrapping paper in contrasting colors, 2.75 cm x 53 cm (1⅛ in. x 21 in.)
- glue stick, pencil, ruler, scissors
- decorative paper

1 Spread a little glue on one piece of paper, about halfway down, and glue the pieces together.

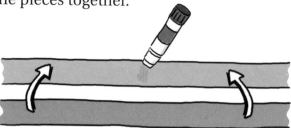

2 Make a mark 24 cm (9½ in.) from one end of the papers. Fold the papers down and across horizontally from that spot.

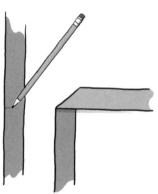

3 Turn the paper so that the point of the fold is at the top.

4 Fold the left side down, to the back, so that the strips meet and a triangle is formed at the top.

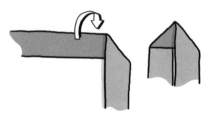

5 Fold the right side strip up, making the side even with the bottom of the triangle.

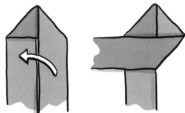

6 Open and re-fold the same strip, keeping the fold in the same direction but moving it backward behind the other strip.

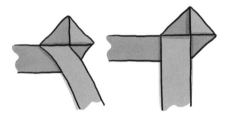

7 Fold the same strip down to the back, making the fold line even with the side. The two strips should be beside each other.

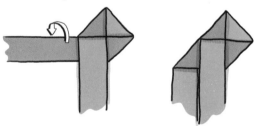

8 Fold the other strip across the front, making the fold line even with the side. Unfold this strip and re-fold it behind the other strip, as you did in step 6.

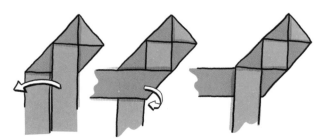

9 Repeat steps 7 and 8 until you reach the end. Trim any excess.

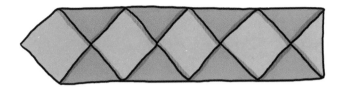

10 Write your message on the decorative paper. Fold it so that it is no more than 2.5 cm (1 in.) wide. Slide it diagonally behind one of the squares.

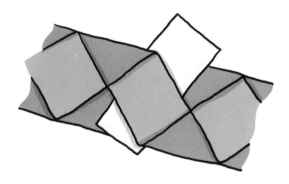

◩ Other Ideas:

Write a series of messages or lines to a poem on separate pieces of paper and slide each into the holder. It can hold up to six messages, three on each side. Number the papers on the outside if you want them to be read in order.

3-D Sign

Make a sign that's bouncy and eye-catching by using woven paper ladders. You'll definitely get your message across!

You will need:

- construction paper in many colors
- magazine or wrapping paper
- a piece of heavy paper or bristol board
- pencil, scissors, ruler, glue stick

1 Decide what letters, words or pictures you want for your sign. Draw and cut out block letters from construction, magazine or wrapping paper. If you want to cut out whole words, draw them so that the letters touch each other. Don't cut between the letters.

2 Cut two strips of construction paper 1 cm x 15 cm (½ in. x 6 in.) in different colors.

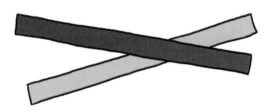

3 Put glue on the end of one strip. Press the other strip onto the glue, holding the strips at a right angle to each other.

4 Fold the front strip to the back. Fold the other strip to the back, over the first. Continue to fold the strips tightly over each other at the back, making a series of overlapping squares. Repeat until you reach the end. Put glue on the inside of the last fold and press it down.

5 Trim any excess paper. Stretch out the paper slightly.

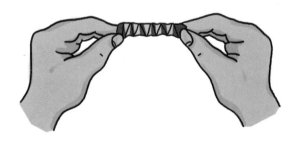

6 Make at least one ladder for each cut letter, word or picture. Long words may need two ladders. Your ladders can be different lengths, so they will bounce at different heights.

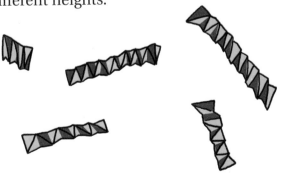

7 Arrange the letters, words and pictures for your sign on the heavy paper or bristol board.

8 Glue a letter, word or picture to one end of a ladder. Glue the other end of the ladder in place on the paper. Repeat with all the pieces. If any of the ladders are too tall, trim and re-glue them. Let your sign dry. Hang it high so that people can read the bouncing words easily.

◣ Other Ideas:

You can also use paper ladders to make bouncing earrings (page 145).

Paper Gluing

One of the best things about paper is how strong it gets when you glue it. There are many different techniques that use paper and glue to make sculptures, art and lots of great gifts. You may already know how to make papier mâché using torn newspaper layers to create shapes. But did you know that you can make amazing papier-mâché objects using tissue paper? You can also make mosaics and collages, creating pictures from torn paper and glue. And in this section, you will also learn how to do decoupage, using paper and glue to decorate objects.

TIPS:

For papier-mâché crafts, you need a paste made with flour and water. Mix 125 mL (½ c.) white flour with 125 mL (½ c.) water. Stir until smooth. Ask an adult to help you slowly pour the mixture into 375 mL (1½ c.) boiling water. Stir and cook for about 5 minutes, until thick and creamy. Pour and stir through a sieve to strain out lumps. Let cool, stirring every few minutes to let the steam escape. The paste will keep covered in the fridge for three to four days.

You can also use wallpaper paste for papier-mâché crafts. Make sure the paste is non-toxic and suitable for crafts. Follow the manufacturer's mixing instructions.

White craft glue is used for many gluing projects. Use non-toxic glue suitable for crafts.

109

Tissue-Paper Bowl

This delicate bowl is made with a papier-mâché technique and layers of tissue paper. It's great for holding jewelry and hair ornaments or wrapped candies.

You will need:

- flour paste (page 109)
- strips of tissue paper — choose colors that blend together well, such as red, yellow, orange or blue, green, yellow
- newspaper, 2 plastic yogurt or margarine containers, white glue, spoon, petroleum jelly, jar or can, glue brush, paper towel
- smooth bowl for a mold
- craft glitter, acrylic paint and paintbrush, varnish or Podge (optional)

1 Cover your work surface with newspaper. Put about 125 mL (½ c.) flour paste into a plastic container. Add about 25 mL (2 tbsp.) white glue and stir well.

2 Cover the outside of the bowl with a thick layer of petroleum jelly. Set it upside down on a jar so that the lip doesn't touch the work surface.

3 Fill the other plastic container with water. Dip a strip of tissue paper in the water. Place it on the bowl. Cover the bowl with a layer of strips dipped in water.

4 Cover with a second layer of dry tissue. Do not dip any of the second layer in water.

5 Put strips of tissue on the newspaper work surface and carefully brush them with paste. Lay them on the bowl, overlapping the pieces as you work over the whole surface. Continue layering with tissue and paste, carefully smoothing down each piece. Gently brush out any air bubbles or bumps.

6 When you have finished about ten layers, let your bowl dry overnight.

7 Remove the tissue bowl from the mold bowl. You may have to run a small, thin knife around the inside to loosen the bowl. Gently wiggle and pull.

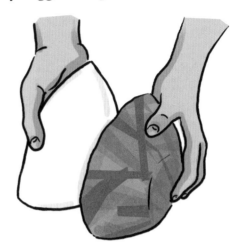

8 Use a piece of paper towel to wipe out the inside of the tissue bowl. Don't worry if a couple pieces of tissue come off.

Instructions continue on the next page ☞

9 Apply a light layer of paste to the inside of the bowl, followed by two layers of tissue. You can apply tissue over the rim to smooth out the edge, or leave the edge ragged. Let dry.

10 After your bowl has dried, decorate with paint or glitter, if you like. You can cover it with a layer of varnish to make it stronger and a bit more transparent.

◢ MARACAS

You can use the tissue papier-mâché technique to make beautiful maracas from old light bulbs. Use the same materials that you did for your tissue-paper bowl.

1 Tear some white bond paper into small pieces.

2 Use the paper and the flour paste (page 109) to cover an old light bulb. (Don't cover the bulb with petroleum jelly.) Apply at least ten layers of paper.

3 Brush strips of tissue paper with paste and cover the white paper with them. Put on at least twenty layers to make the covering very thick.

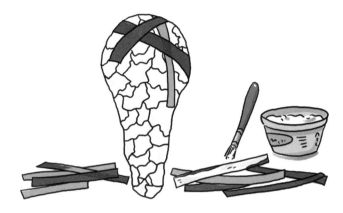

4 Let your maraca dry thoroughly. This may take a few days.

5 When you're sure it's dry, hit the maraca on the edge of a table. The light bulb will break and make a great rattling sound when you shake it. Cover with varnish.

◤ Other Ideas:

Use scraps of interesting papers throughout your pasting process. Bits of Japanese, origami, or wrapping papers make great designs.

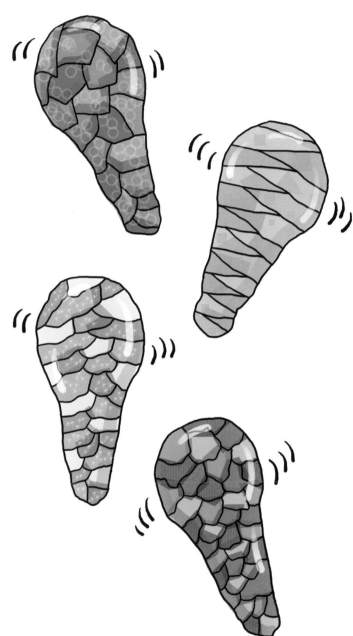

Rock Cast Box

Make an unusual papier-mâché box for small treasures. Find an interestingly shaped rock to use as the form for your box.

◣ You will need:

- a rock, about 15 cm (6 in.) long
- flour paste (page 109)
- small pieces of white bond paper
- strips of tissue paper,
  about 1 cm x 7.5 cm (½ in. x 3 in.)
- varnish or Podge and brush (optional)
- newspaper, 2 plastic yogurt or margarine containers, white glue, spoon, petroleum jelly, cookie sheet, glue brush, X-Acto or craft knife.

1 Cover your work surface with newspaper. Put about 125 mL (½ c.) flour paste into a plastic container. Add about 25 mL (2 tbsp.) white glue and stir well.

2 Cover your rock with a thick layer of petroleum jelly. Place it on the cookie sheet.

3 Fill a plastic container with water. Dip a piece of white paper in the water. Place it on the rock. Cover the surface of the rock, overlapping the papers.

4 Brush a bit of paste onto the covered rock surface. Layer pieces of white paper and paste. Gently brush out any air bubbles or bumps.

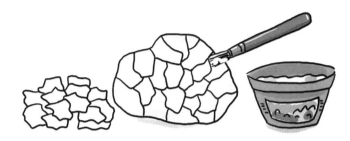

5 After you have about four layers of white paper, layer strips of tissue paper, spreading paste and pressing down the strips with the brush.

6 When you have finished about twenty layers, put your box on a cooling rack to dry overnight or longer depending on the size of the rock.

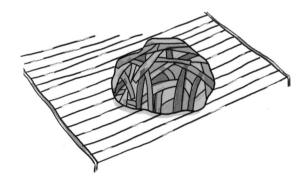

7 Draw a line around the sides of the box where you want it to separate into a top and bottom. Use an X-Acto knife to cut through all layers along this line.

8 Gently remove the box from the rock mold. You may have to gently run a knife along the inside to loosen the rock.

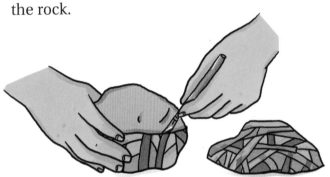

9 Use a piece of paper towel to wipe out the inside of the box. Remove any loose pieces of paper. Cover with varnish, if you like.

Tissue-Paper Vase

This is an easy way to make an elegant vase for your crepe-paper roses (page 80) or tissue flowers (page 82). If you cover the vase with varnish, you can also use it with real flowers.

◤ You will need:

- tissue paper in a variety of colors
- a clean, empty glass bottle or jar
- varnish or Podge and brush (optional)
- newspaper, scissors (optional), white glue and spoon, plastic yogurt or margarine container, glue brush

1 Cover your work surface with newspaper. Cut or tear tissue paper into small, irregularly shaped pieces between 1 cm and 5 cm in size (½ in. and 2 in.). Your vase will look very different depending on whether you cut or tear the paper, so you may want to experiment with each method.

2 Mix 25 mL (2 tbsp.) white glue and 10 mL (2 tsp.) water in the plastic container. Brush a light coating of glue onto a small section of the bottle. Put pieces of tissue paper over the glued area, slightly overlapping them and smoothing down the edges with the glue brush.

3 Continue to brush on glue and add paper until the bottle is covered. Let dry.

4 If you want to make your vase waterproof and the colors more permanent, cover with varnish.

◩ Other Ideas:

● You can use the same technique to cover blown Easter eggs. Tear the tissue paper into very small pieces and pick up each piece with your glue brush, coated with glue. Carefully place the tissue on the egg and gently brush down.

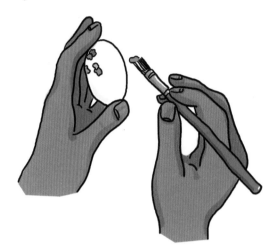

● Cover Styrofoam balls with this technique and use them for ornaments. They will have a beautiful stained-glass look.

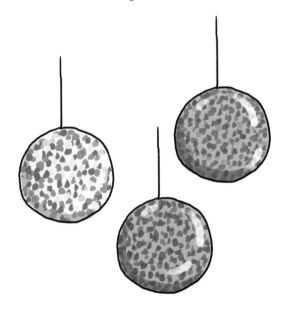

Mosaics

People have made mosaics for more than 3000 years, using pieces of broken pottery, tile or glass to create pictures. You can use scraps of colorful paper left over from other projects to make a simple butterfly mosaic for a card.

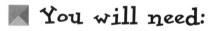

You will need:

- small pieces of colored paper
- a piece of black construction or art paper, 16 cm x 25 cm (6½ in. x 10 in.)
- scissors, pencil, white glue and glue brush or glue stick

1 Cut the colored paper scraps into small, irregularly shaped pieces. Put the pieces into piles sorted by color.

2 Fold the black paper in half widthwise.

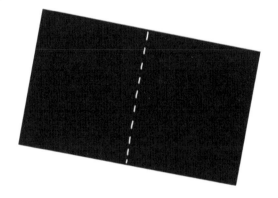

3 Lightly draw the outline of a butterfly on the paper. Draw an outline for each different area of color.

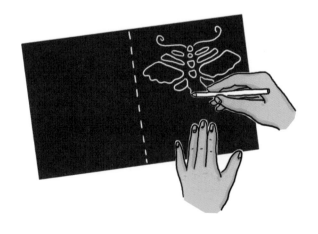

4 Pick a piece of colored paper to fit along the edge of your design or trim one to fit. Glue it to your design. Leaving about 0.25 cm (⅛ in.), trim and glue the next piece in place.

5 Continue filling in the picture, trimming pieces of paper as needed to make the details of your picture. Let dry.

Other Ideas:

● Make a bowl of flowers. Draw a bowl, the flowers, the leaves and stems, and fill each in with a different color.

● Design a whole landscape or sunset. Plan a simple design with shapes to fill with colors.

● Look in magazines for picture ideas and trace or copy the areas of color. Make an impressionist picture by gluing bits of colored paper into areas.

Aquarium Collage

Half the fun of making a collage is going through old magazines and papers and finding unusual pictures to cut. Your collage will be a great backing to an aquarium.

◤ You will need:

- an aquarium
- blue construction paper
- gray or dark green paper
- old magazines or scraps from colored papers
- scissors, glue stick, adhesive putty

1 Cut down or glue together blue construction paper so that it is long enough to cover the back of your aquarium.

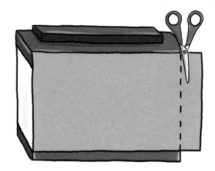

2 Cut down or glue the gray or green paper so that it is as long as the back of your aquarium. Tear it about 7 cm (2¾ in.) wide with an irregular edge to make the sea floor. Glue it to the backing paper.

3 Cut fish and plants from magazines or colored paper. You can cut actual pictures from magazines, or cut the shapes of fish and plants from colored paper.

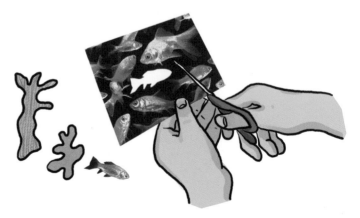

4 Glue the fish and plants to the background. Put some fish behind plants and others in front. Let dry.

5 Put little pieces of adhesive putty in each corner of the front of the picture. Press the collage to the back of the aquarium, leaving a small space between the paper and the glass. This will make sure that condensation from the aquarium doesn't damage your picture.

◣ Other Ideas:

● A portrait collage shows someone's personality through photographs and pictures. Make one as a gift for someone. Cut out pictures from magazines of things that remind you of that person. Add cut photos and other mementos.

● Cut out the letters of your name from wrapping paper. Collage them with pictures of yourself and the things you like to do.

Double Picture Frame

This folded picture frame holds two vertical 10 cm x 15 cm (4 in. x 6 in.) pictures. It can stand to show the pictures or be folded to store them.

◢ You will need:

- a piece of decorative or wrapping paper, 23 cm x 34 cm (9 in. x 13½ in.)

- 4 pieces of thin cardboard, 15 cm x 20 cm (6 in. x 8 in.)

- 2 pieces of decorative or wrapping paper, 18 cm x 23 cm (7 in. x 9 in.)

- a piece of contrasting paper, 19 cm x 30 cm (7½ in. x 12 in.)

- pencil, ruler, white glue, spoon, plastic yogurt or margarine container, newspaper, glue brush, wax paper, X-Acto or craft knife, scissors, cutting board

1 On the wrong side of the large piece of decorative paper, draw a 1 cm (½ in.) margin around all four sides. Draw a line 16 cm (6½ in.) from each side to form a 1 cm (½ in.) space down the middle of the page.

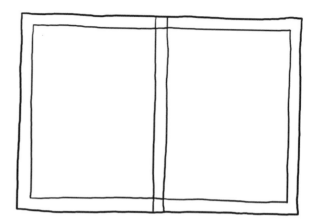

2 Mix 10 mL (2 tsp.) glue with a few drops of water in the plastic container. Place the paper face down on newspaper and cover it with the glue mixture, avoiding the 1 cm (½ in.) space in the center. Make sure the glue goes to the edges of the paper.

3 Place two pieces of cardboard on the paper, matching the top, side, and bottom edges of each to the margin lines. Fold over the corners of the paper as shown.

4 Spread glue mixture on the folded corners. Fold over the margin along all sides. This is the backing for your frames. Put it between sheets of wax paper and place under heavy books until dry.

5 Draw a 2.75 cm (1⅛ in.) margin around the sides of a piece of cardboard. Use an X-Acto knife to cut out the inside rectangle. Repeat with the last piece of cardboard.

6 On the wrong side of one of the smaller pieces of decorative paper, draw a margin 5 cm (2 in.) from the top, side and bottom edges. Use the X-Acto knife to cut out this rectangle. Repeat with the other piece of paper.

Instructions continue on the next page ☞

7 Draw a margin on one of these paper frames 1 cm (½ in.) from the top, side and bottom. Place it face down on newspaper and spread glue mixture over the entire page. Put a cardboard frame inside the margin area.

8 Fold over the corners of the paper as shown. Spread more glue mixture on the folded corners and fold over the margins.

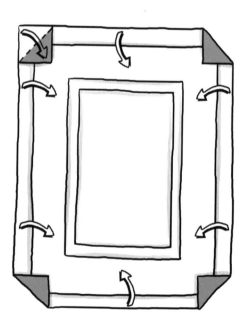

9 Make a diagonal cut on the paper from the inside of each corner to the cardboard. Fold over these inside margins. Put the frame between sheets of wax paper and place under heavy books until dry.

10 Repeat steps 7 to 9 for the second frame.

11 Spread glue mixture over the back of the contrasting paper. Lay it down on the front of the frame back, leaving a 0.5 cm (¼ in.) margin around all sides.

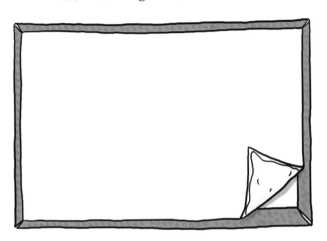

12 Run a thin line of full-strength glue on the back of the frame fronts, along the bottom and sides. Put the glue right at the edge. Don't put any along the top. Press the frame fronts onto the backing, matching the bottom and sides.

13 Put the double frame between sheets of wax paper and place under heavy books until dry.

14 Slide your pictures into the frames from the top.

Single Picture Frame

This picture frame will hold one 10 cm x 15 cm (4 in. x 6 in.) picture either horizontally or vertically.

◥ You will need:

- 2 pieces of decorative or wrapping paper, 18 cm x 23 cm (7 in. x 9 in.)
- 2 pieces of thin cardboard, 15 cm x 20 cm (6 in. x 8 in.)
- a piece of contrasting paper, 14 cm x 19 cm (5½ in. x 7½ in.)
- yarn or thin fabric ribbon, 25 cm (10 in.) long
- pencil, ruler, white glue, spoon, plastic yogurt or margarine container, newspapers, glue brush, wax paper, X-Acto or craft knife, cutting board, hammer, nail and block of wood to hammer into, scissors

1 Draw a 1 cm (½ in.) margin around the wrong side of your decorative paper.

2 Using the two pieces of cardboard, follow steps 2 to 9 and step 11 on pages 122–125.

3 Use the hammer and nail to make two small holes on the frame back, 1 cm (½ in.) from the sides. If you are using your frame for a horizontal picture, put the holes 5 cm (2 in.) from the top. If you are using it vertically, put the holes 7 cm (2 ¾ in.) from the top.

4 Pull the yarn through one hole from the back to the front. Hold 2.5 cm (1 in.) of the end of the yarn along the margin. Thread the other end through the other hole. Pull gently until tight. Trim, leaving 2.5 cm (1 in.) of yarn at each side.

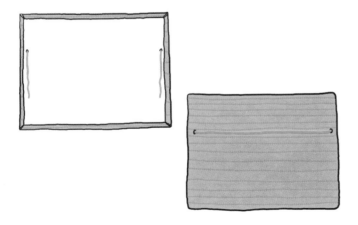

5 Follow step 12 on page 125, putting extra glue on the yarn and keeping it along the margin. Put the frame between sheets of wax paper and place under heavy books until dry.

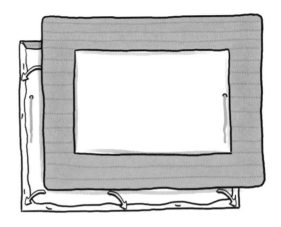

6 Slide your picture into the frame from the top.

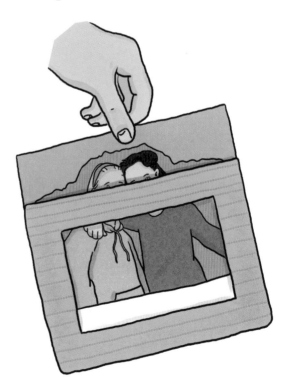

Star Book

This unusual book opens out into a star.
Without covers, it makes a unique card.

◢ You will need:

- 4 squares of bond or origami paper,
  all the same color, 10 cm x 10 cm (4 in. x 4 in.)
- a square of wrapping paper,
  8 cm x 8 cm (3 in. x 3 in.)
- satin ribbon, 0.5 cm x 30 cm (¼ in. x 12 in.)
- a pen or pencil
- 2 squares of matboard, 5 cm x 5 cm (2 in. x 2 in.)
- newspaper, glue stick, wax paper

1 Fold one square of bond paper in half diagonally. Open it.

2 Turn the paper to the wrong side. Fold it in half. Open it and turn. Fold it in half the other way and open.

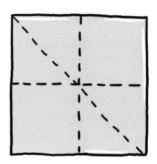

3 With the paper facing you in a diamond shape, push the diagonal folds in to meet each other at the center. Turn it, and you should have an unfolded square facing you. Sharpen all folds (page 8). Repeat steps 1 to 3 with each paper.

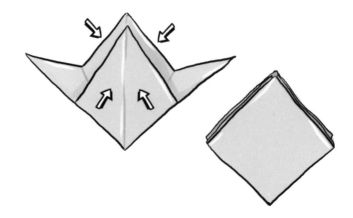

4 Open one paper with the good side facing you. Place it on newspaper and spread glue on only the two unfolded sections.

5 Press an unfolded section of a folded second paper onto the glued portion of the first, matching the folded corners.

6 Press a third paper onto the other glued section of the first.

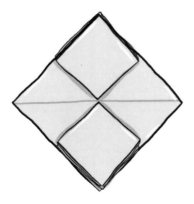

7 Spread glue on one side of the last folded square. Press it onto one of the other folded squares, with the folded corners meeting at the center.

8 Fold the flat paper up into a square to match the others. Put all of the glued papers between sheets of wax paper and place under heavy books until dry.

9 Open your star carefully and write a message in each of the folded sections, if you like. Do not write on the outside sections.

Instructions continue on the next page ☞

10 Fold the ribbon in half. Starting 0.5 cm (¼ in.) from the fold, spread glue along 2.5 cm (1 in.) of the ribbon. Attach this glued portion diagonally to the top paper. Repeat with the other half of the ribbon, gluing it to the back of the folded squares. Make sure you leave 0.5 cm (¼ in.) of the folded ribbon unattached. Let dry.

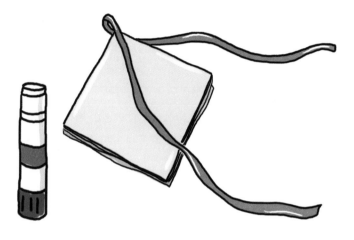

11 Cover each matboard separately with wrapping paper to make the covers. See steps 2 to 4, page 122.

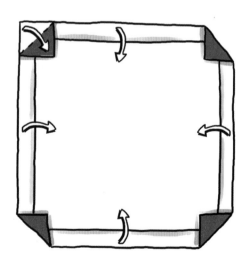

12 Glue the covers to both ends of the closed papers. Put the book between sheets of wax paper and place under heavy books until dry.

13 Open your star by putting the front and back together and tying the ribbon.

Decoupage

Decoupage is a great way to make ordinary objects such as bottles, boxes and trays look special by covering them with cut-paper decorations.

◣ You will need:

- an object to decoupage, such as a small wooden box, old metal tray or wooden fruit basket

- acrylic paint and paintbrush (optional)

- old greeting cards, photos, strong wrapping paper, old calendar pictures, photocopied images or computer art (don't use magazine pictures — the paper is too thin)

- fine-grain sandpaper, a clean cloth or tea towel, small, sharp scissors, such as nail scissors, varnish or Podge and a spoon, small plastic yogurt or margarine container, glue brush, newspaper

1 Lightly sand your object, making it as smooth and clean as possible. Wipe it thoroughly with a slightly damp cloth.

2 Paint your object with acrylic paint, if you like. Let dry.

3 Cut out the pictures you want to use. Trim them so there is no background or white area showing.

4 Plan the placement of pictures. You can completely cover your object or place just a few pictures in interesting places. Pictures can be folded over the sides of a box or the edges of a tray.

Instructions continue on the next page ☞

5 Mix 10 mL (2 tsp.) varnish with 5 mL (1 tsp.) water in the plastic container. Spread a thin layer over the object. Let dry completely.

6 Make a slightly thicker mixture with 20 mL (4 tsp.) varnish and 5 mL (1 tsp.) water in the plastic container. Spread a layer over the object.

7 Place one of your pictures on newspaper, face down. Paint the back with the thicker mixture. Lift it carefully and put it down on your object.

8 Paint the thicker mixture over the picture, pressing hard with the brush to smooth out all bumps and firmly attach the edges. If the edges of the paper begin to curl, paint them with full-strength varnish.

9 Repeat to attach all the pictures. Finish with a layer of varnish over the whole object. Let dry.

10 Lightly sand the surface. Wipe with a slightly damp cloth. Cover with a layer of varnish. Repeat sanding and varnishing until the surface is completely smooth.

◤ Other Ideas:

● Use some of the designs from your paper-cutting projects (page 56) for your decoupage.

● Decoupage a Kirigami design (page 66) onto an old metal tray and paint the words of a Japanese haiku poem around the edge.

● Decoupage a name silhouette (page 62) onto a painted board to make a permanent sign or frame.

● Decoupage cut valentine's hearts (page 60) onto a painted wooden basket and fill it with chocolates.

Beads

You can use magazine paper or scraps of wrapping paper to make decorative beads in many sizes and shapes. It's a great way to make necklaces, bracelets and earrings to match!

◤ You will need:

- wrapping or magazine paper
- varnish or Podge and brush (optional)
- scissors (optional), petroleum jelly, knitting needles or skewers in various sizes, white glue, spoon, plastic yogurt or margarine container, glue brush, newspaper
- beading thread or elastic

1 Cut or tear strips of paper into shapes as shown. The pieces should be 30 cm to 60 cm (12 in. to 24 in.) long and 2 cm to 5 cm (¾ in. to 2 in.) wide.

2 Spread some petroleum jelly on a knitting needle or skewer to keep the bead from sticking.

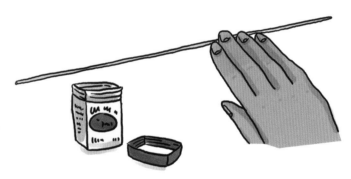

3 Mix 25 mL (2 tbsp.) glue with a couple of drops of water in the plastic container.

4 Put a strip face down on newspaper. Spread a light layer of glue along the strip.

5 Curl the wide end of the paper around the needle. Wind the paper around itself until you reach the end. Smooth it out as you go so that it is tight and even. Press down the end. Add a drop of glue to hold the end down, if needed.

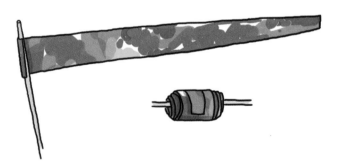

6 Hold the bead and gently slip it off the needle. Let dry. If you want to make the bead glossy, cover with varnish. Repeat to make more beads.

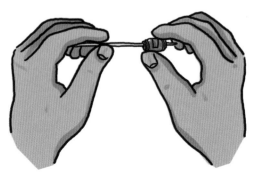

7 Thread your beads onto beading thread or thin elastic to make a necklace or bracelet.

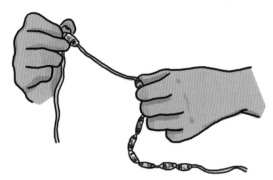

Other Ideas:

● Change the design of your beads by using different sizes of paper, varying the angles of cut, tearing the edges or layering papers.

● Make earrings by threading a needle with beading or metallic thread and tying a plastic bead on the end. Thread on the paper bead, slip another plastic bead onto the needle, then thread the needle through an earring hook. Go back down through the top plastic bead, then the paper bead, then the bottom plastic bead. Knot both ends of the thread together and trim.

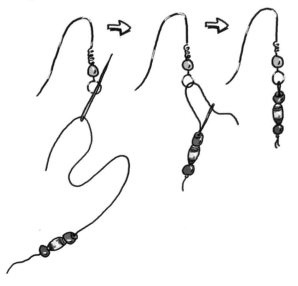

135

Paper-Twine Earring Jar

Paper twine made from crepe paper can be used for many crafts. This project wraps twine around a can to make a decorative earring container.

◤ You will need:

- a clean, small, empty tin can with one end removed
- 2 pieces of colored bond or art paper
- crepe-paper streamers
- tape, ruler, string, pencil, scissors, newspaper, white glue, glue brush

1 Fold a piece of tape over the edge of the can to prevent you from getting cut.

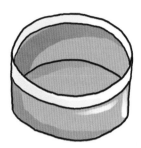

2 Measure the width of the can by wrapping a piece of string around it, then measuring the length of the string. Measure the height of the can. Cut a piece of colored paper that is the length of the string plus 2.5 cm (1 in.) and the height of the can plus 0.5 cm (¼ in.).

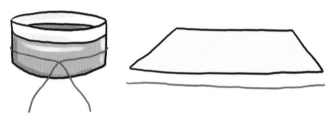

3 Place a piece of the paper on newspaper and cover with glue.

4 Put the paper inside the can, pushing it to the sides and pressing down the overlap. Fold the top over the edge of the can.

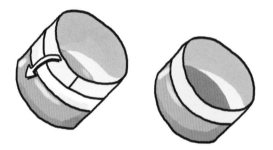

5 Place the can on a piece of colored paper. Trace around the bottom. Cut this circle out.

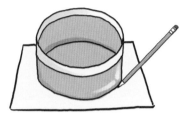

6 Push the circle to the bottom of the can. You don't need to glue it in place.

7 Put a line of glue around the top of the can. Twist a streamer tightly to begin the twine. Wind the twine around the top. Continue twisting and winding around the can, placing each row snug to the one before. Secure with drops of glue.

8 Change the color of the crepe paper at any time. Simply break the paper off, glue it in place and begin with the new color. If the crepe paper gets tangled, reverse the direction that you are twisting. Put a drop of glue down with each change of direction.

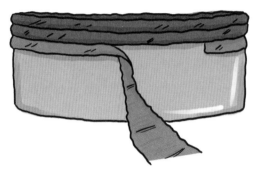

9 When you reach the bottom of the can, put a line of glue along the base to hold the twine in place.

◥ Other Ideas:

● Wrap paper twine around a shaped glass jar to make a vase or pencil jar.

● Wrap twine around a barrette form to make a decorative barrette.

● Use paper twine instead of ribbon at the base of a pom-pom or fan (page 144).

Party Cracker

Use these festive crackers for any special occasion. You can fill them with crafts that you have made, such as a diary necklace (page 28), barrettes (page 144), fan earrings (page 38) or puffy stars (page 14). Write your own mottoes or fortunes to include inside.

◤ You will need:

- a piece of wrapping paper,
  6.5 cm x 27 cm (2½ in. x 11 in.)
- 2 pieces of tissue paper, 27 cm x 40 cm (11 in. x 16 in.)
- glitter glue and/or craft glitter
- cracker snaps (available at hobby and craft stores)
- a paper towel roll, cut to 20 cm (8 in.)
- small gifts, candies and fortunes
- 2 pieces of ribbon, 30 cm (12 in.) long
- decorative-edge scissors (optional), white glue

1 Trim the wrapping paper with decorative-edge scissors, if you like.

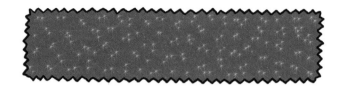

2 Lay the tissue paper flat, one piece on top of the other. Glue the strip of wrapping paper widthwise down the middle of the tissue paper. Use glitter glue to decorate the rest of the tissue. Let dry.

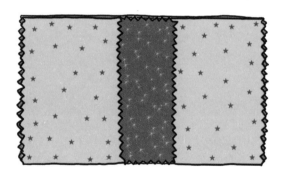

3 Slide the cracker snap through the tube. Make sure that it sticks out evenly at both ends. Put small gifts, candies and fortunes in the tube.

4 Turn the papers over. Spread a layer of glue along the length of the paper towel roll. Position the roll in the middle of one edge of the tissue.

5 Roll the tissue paper around the tube. Glue the end of the paper in place, gluing down both layers.

6 Wrap a ribbon around the tissue paper at each end. Tighten and tie in a double knot and bow.

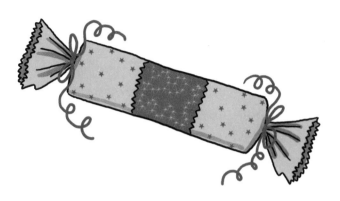

◤ Other Ideas:

Make a simple paper hat to put in your party cracker. Glue two pieces of tissue paper, 12 cm x 32 cm (4½ in. x 12½ in.), together at the sides. Let dry. Fold the tissue in half three times to get a thin rectangle. Draw on a simple crown shape, as shown. Cut, open and decorate with stickers or glitter glue.

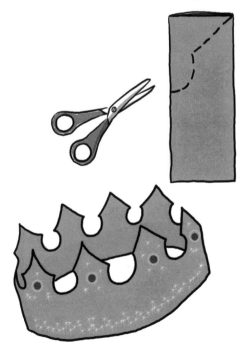

Wreath

This spring wreath can be made for any season — just change the colors of the flowers. You could easily substitute roses (page 80) or pom-poms (page 83), or add butterflies (page 30). Add on other decorations such as artificial berries or bows.

◣ You will need:

- a coat hanger
- newspaper
- crepe-paper streamers in green, orange, pink, purple
- heavy green thread or floral wire
- scissors, masking tape, clear tape, white glue

1 Stretch the coat hanger into a circle, leaving the hook at the top.

2 Cut newspaper into strips 10 cm (4 in.) wide. Fold a strip in half lengthwise and wind it around the circle, taping it in place with masking tape. Continue winding strips, covering the wire until you have two layers. Leave the hook uncovered.

3 Wind green crepe paper around the circle, completely covering the newspaper. Attach it with clear tape.

4 Fold over 10 cm (4 in.) of a green streamer. Hold this between your fingers and wind over nine layers. Cut off and trim to a leaf shape, cutting through all layers. Repeat ten times, so that you have 100 leaves.

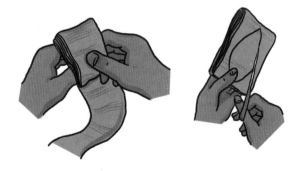

5 Shape the leaves by gently pulling your thumb along the center of the leaf, stretching the middle. Bunch three leaves side by side and twist the bottoms together. Repeat with the other leaves.

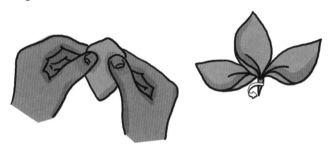

6 Glue the bottom of a leaf group to the wreath. Add leaves, placing them so that they point both to the outside and the inside of the circle. Cut and add more leaves if necessary to make your wreath look full.

7 To make flowers, begin by tightly rolling an orange, pink or purple streamer into a cylinder. Continue rolling more loosely until it's about 1 cm to 2.5 cm (½ in. to 1 in.) in diameter.

8 Tie thread tightly around the roll, about 1 cm (½ in.) from the bottom. Leave an end 20 cm (8 in.) long.

9 Tap the top of the flower on a table, squishing the "petals" slightly. Stretch and push the petals, gently opening the flower bud. Make at least twelve flowers in different colors and sizes.

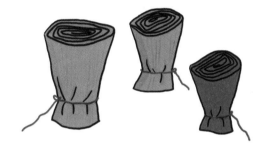

10 Tie on the flowers by winding the end of the thread around the wreath and knotting it. Glue a couple of extra leaves to the base of each flower.

Pencil Pot

Use a scrap of wrapping paper and paper in a contrasting color to make this simple holder for pencils, markers or paintbrushes.

◢ You will need:

- a clean, empty tin can with one end removed
- wrapping or other decorative paper
- colored paper in a contrasting color
- tape, string, pencil, ruler, scissors, white glue, spoon, plastic yogurt or margarine container, newspaper, glue brush

1 Fold a piece of tape over the edge of the can to prevent you from getting cut or scratched. It will also keep the paper on the edge of your pencil pot smooth.

2 Measure the width of the can by wrapping a piece of string around it, then marking and measuring the length. Measure the height of the can.

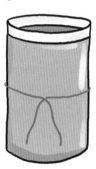

3 Cut a piece of wrapping paper that is twice as long as the length of the string. Make it the height of the can plus 0.5 cm (¼ in.).

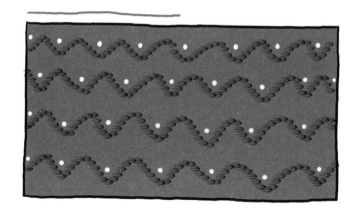

4 Mix 25 mL (2 tbsp.) glue with a few drops of water in the plastic container. Put the wrapping paper face down on newspaper. Spread glue mixture over the back of the paper, right to the edges.

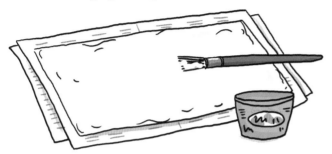

5 Place the can so that the bottom edge is even with the bottom of the wrapping paper. Carefully roll the paper tightly around the can, trying to keep the bottom edge even. Allow the paper to overlap until you get to the end. Press it in place.

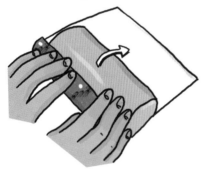

6 Push the edge of the paper inside the can. Press in place.

7 Cut the colored paper the length of the piece of string and the height of the can minus 1 cm (½ in.). Cover it with glue.

8 Place the colored paper inside the can, pushing it to the sides and pressing down the overlap.

9 Place the can on a piece of colored paper. Trace around the bottom. Cut this circle out.

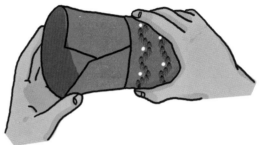

10 Push the circle to the bottom of the can. You don't need to glue it in place.

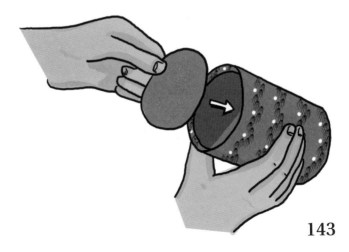

Barrette

You can use crafts from this book, such as pom-poms (page 83), tiny butterflies (page 31), fans (page 38) or tissue flowers (page 82), to make a bouncy hair barrette.

◢ You will need:

- paper objects to put on barrette
- beading or metallic thread
- fabric ribbon for each pom-pom, fan or flower 15 cm (6 in.) long
- a metal barrette form
- white glue, tacky or super hold

1 Decide how many pom-poms, butterflies, fans or flowers you want to put on the barrette.

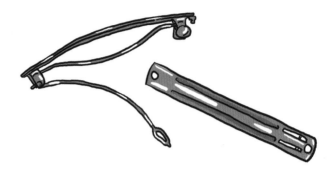

2 Cut a piece of thread 25 cm (10 in.) long. Tie it around the paper object and knot tightly. If you are using a pom-pom, fan or flower, tie the thread around the base. If you are using a butterfly, tie it around the middle.

3 Tie ribbon or paper twine (page 136) around the bottom of pom-poms, fans or flowers, over the knotted thread.

4 Put a coating of glue along the back surface of the barrette.

5 Push the paper object down into the glue and wind the thread around the back section of the barrette. Knot the thread. Repeat with each object.

6 Put a line of white glue along the threads, where they connect to the object. Let dry.

EARRINGS

Use earring hooks and thin nylon or beading thread (available at craft or hobby stores) to make earrings from paper crafts. Double the thread and knot it before you start.

Puffy Stars (page 14): Sew through the star from one side up through the opposite point. Loop the thread around the ring of an earring hook several times. Go back down through the star and knot the threads together at the bottom. Tie on decorative beads and trim.

Ladder Earrings (page 106): Make your ladders from metallic or wrapping paper. Sew up through the ladder from the bottom to the top. Finish as with Puffy Stars.

Butterflies (page 30): Tie the thread around the middle of a miniature butterfly, loop it through an earring hook, pull tight and go around the ring twice. Go around the butterfly again and tie the ends together. Secure with a drop of glue.

Paper Making

Paper was originally made by mashing up rags, plants, tree bark and old fishing nets into a wet pulp that was dried flat on screens. Today, paper mills make tons of pulp daily, using trees that have been grown especially for making paper. You can make your own pulp for paper and paper ornaments by recycling used paper and paper scraps. And you'll do it almost exactly the same way as the Chinese first did, 2000 years ago.

TIPS:

Paper pulp is made by soaking paper scraps and then blending them with water into very tiny pieces. Use a blender and ask an adult to help you.

The kind of paper you choose is important. Avoid construction paper, newsprint or magazine paper. Use an assortment of interesting art paper scraps or leftover pieces of origami or wrapping papers. Try using old envelopes.

Never throw leftover pulp down the sink.

Handmade Paper

To make paper, you must have a dipping tray with a screen to strain the pulp. This project shows you how to make one out of a recycled plastic-foam food tray.

◢ You will need:

- scraps of paper
- a clean plastic-foam tray, such as a meat or vegetable tray, or an old wooden frame
- nylon screening, cut to fit inside the lip of the tray or edges of the frame
- fabric dye or food coloring (optional)
- plastic yogurt or margarine container, X-Acto or craft knife, cutting board, duct tape, scissors, plastic washtub or dish pan, hand blender or blender, 4 to 8 towels, sponge, rolling pin, sieve

1 Tear paper into small pieces about 5 cm x 5 cm (2 in. x 2 in.) square. You'll need a total of about 500 mL (2 c.), packed, of torn paper. Put the pieces in the plastic container, fill with water and let soak for 30 minutes.

2 If you are using a foam tray, cut out the middle with an X-Acto knife, leaving a 2.5 cm (1 in.) border around the edges.

3 Attach the screening with duct tape around all four sides of the tray or frame.

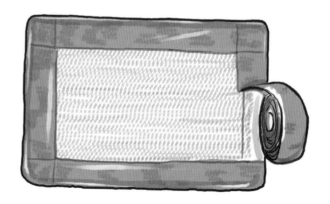

4 Fill the washtub half full with water.

5 Ask an adult to help you to blend the paper. Put a hand blender in the container and blend until it is the consistency of porridge. Pour it into the washtub. Alternatively, put small amounts of the torn paper in a blender, mix and put each batch of paper pulp into the washtub.

6 Use your hands to thoroughly mix the water and paper pulp. Add any decorative elements you want. (See "Other Ideas," page 150 for suggestions.) Color your paper, if you want, by adding fabric dye or food coloring.

7 Slip the dipping screen into the water, under the floating pulp. Dip it with the edges face down. Lift it straight up, catching a thin layer of pulp on the screen. Jiggle the pulp around to even it out on the screen and let the water drain through.

8 Flip the screen over onto a flat towel. Pat the back of the screen with a sponge to soak up excess water. Wring out the sponge in the sink, then continue patting and soaking up as much excess water as you can. Lift the screen off and place another towel on top.

9 Roll over the towel with the rolling pin, squishing out as much water as possible.

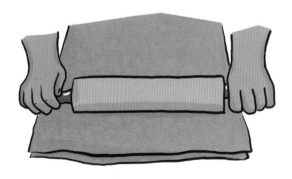

Instructions continue on the next page ☞

10 Remove the towel and gently lift off the paper. Place it between fresh towels to dry overnight, or dry it in the microwave. To do this, carefully place the wet paper on a piece of paper towel. Set your microwave on low for 1 minute and check the paper. Depending on your microwave, you may need to "cook" it for 1 to 4 minutes. Don't dry it in your microwave if it has metallic paper in it.

11 Repeat steps 7 to 10, using dry towels when necessary. Stack papers and fold the sides of the towels over top. Your 500 mL (2 c.) of torn paper will make about six to eight pieces of handmade paper.

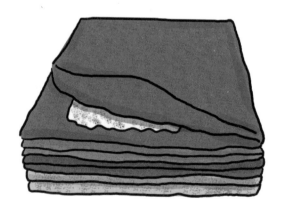

12 When you are finished, strain the water through a sieve and pour the excess pulp into the garbage.

Other Ideas:

● Add decorations to your paper to make it interesting. Try adding dried flowers or leaves, confetti or craft glitter to the pulp. Add some sweet spices such as crushed whole cloves, grated nutmeg or a broken vanilla bean to get scented paper.

● Fold the finished paper in half and attach a decoration to the front, such as paper-twine tied into a bow (page 136), kimono (page 36) or fan (page 38), to make a special card. To make a matching envelope, you will need to make a larger dipping tray.

Stationery Folder

Make this simple folder to hold your handmade notepaper or cards.

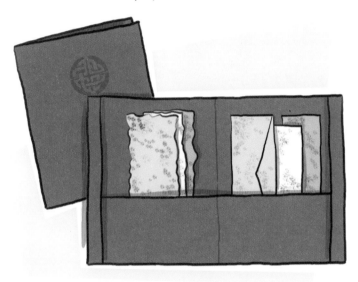

You will need:

- a piece of heavy art paper or card stock, 42 cm x 53.5 cm (16½ in. x 21 in.)
- pencil, ruler, scissors, glue stick

1 Score (page 8) two lines 2.5 cm (1 in.) from each of the short sides of the paper and fold these to the inside.

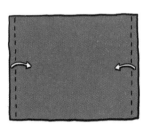

2 Fold the whole sheet in half widthwise, keeping side sections folded. Open it.

3 Score a line 27 cm (11 in.) from the top. Fold it and open.

4 Open the side folds. Cut off the rectangles as shown. Fold up the bottom section.

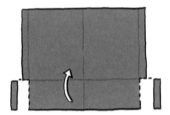

5 Spread glue along the side flaps. Fold over and press down.

6 Decorate the front with collage (page 120), stickers, glitter glue, a paper medallion (page 152) or a cutout shape (page 56).

151

Paper Medallion

This is a quick and easy way to make paper. The small medallion can be used as an ornament, a potpourri (page 157) or a small note card.

You will need:

- toilet paper
- glitter, confetti, small petals from dried flowers, tiny scraps of shiny paper (optional)
- a square of screening, 13 cm x 13 cm (5 in. x 5 in.), or large enough to cover the mouth of the jar
- widemouthed jar with lid, elastic band, 5 small towels, sponge, rolling pin, paper towel (optional), scissors, hole punch (optional)

1 Put six sheets of toilet paper into the jar and fill with water. Add glitter, confetti, dried flowers, shiny paper or other decorative elements, if you like. Screw the lid on tightly and shake well.

2 Remove the lid. Place the screening over the jar and secure with an elastic band.

3 Turn the jar upside down to drain out the water. Jiggle the jar so that all the water runs out and the pulp covers the screen.

4 With the jar still upside down, remove the screening. Place it, with the paper pulp, on a flat towel. Put another towel on top and carefully flip the screening and paper pulp over. Remove the top towel.

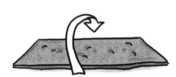

5 Gently pat the back of the screening with the sponge to soak up excess water and even out the paper pulp. Wring out the sponge in the sink, then continue patting and soaking up as much as you can. Remove the screen.

6 Carefully place the paper on a dry towel. Put another towel on top. Roll over it with a rolling pin, squishing out more water.

7 Remove the towel and gently lift off the paper medallion. Place it on a fresh towel to dry overnight, or dry it in the microwave. See step 10, page 150. Don't dry it in your microwave if it has metallic paper in it.

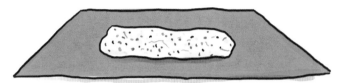

8 When your paper medallion is dry, it can be cut into a shape such as a heart or star. Punch a hole in the top to hang it.

◥ Other Ideas:

● A thicker medallion can be made by repeating the process, stacking up to six circles and pressing them all together (at step 4).

● Add food coloring to the water in step 1 to color your paper.

Pulp Ornaments

By adding glue to strained paper pulp, you can make these fun ornaments or jewelry. They work best when made with cookie cutters that have no back.

◤ You will need:

- scraps of paper
- acrylic paint and paintbrush
- plastic yogurt or margarine container, hand blender or blender, small saucepan, cooking spoon, sieve, white glue, cookie cutters, tea towel, paper towel, toothpick, metal cooling rack

1 Using about 250 mL (1 c.) packed, torn paper, make paper pulp (steps 1 and 5 page 148). Soak for an hour before blending.

2 Put the pulp into the saucepan and ask an adult to help you to bring it to a boil. Stir and cook for 3 minutes. Let cool.

3 Strain the pulp and water through a sieve. Squeeze out all the excess water. Put the pulp back into the plastic container.

4 Add about 50 mL (¼ c.) white glue to the pulp. Mix thoroughly.

5 Place the cookie cutter on a towel and press about 5 mL (1 tsp.) pulp into it. Smooth the pulp to the edges of the shape. Press the pulp down so that it is only about 0.25 cm (⅛ in.) thick. Use paper towel to soak up the excess water.

6 Gently remove the cutter.

7 Use a toothpick to make a hole in the top of the ornament.

8 Repeat with the other cookie cutters until the pulp is used up.

9 When the ornaments are partially dry, gently peel them away from the towel and place them on the cooling rack. They will take at least 24 hours to dry. Or dry them in the microwave. Cook on low for 2 minutes. Check them and gently press them down with a paper towel if they have puffed up. Cook for another 2 minutes.

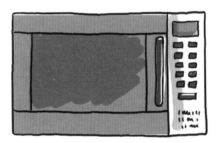

10 Paint your ornaments with acrylic paint and tie a ribbon through each hole.

155

MAKING THINGS WITH PAPER PULP

You can make a lot of different things with paper pulp. Use the recipe on page 154–155, steps 1 to 4.

- Use a candy mold to make ornaments. Spray the mold with a layer of cooking-oil spray and press in the wet pulp. Gently pull it out of the mold to dry.

- Instead of putting a hole in your ornament, glue on a magnetic strip to make a fridge magnet. Use epoxy glue to hold the magnet tightly.

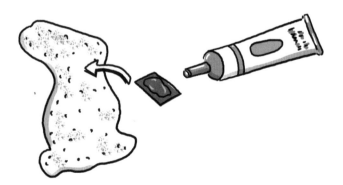

- Use paper pulp to make a bracelet. Cut a piece of a cardboard tube so that it fits easily over your wrist with room to spare.

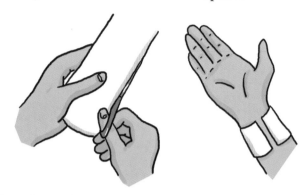

Pat the pulp onto the cardboard, smoothing around all surfaces.

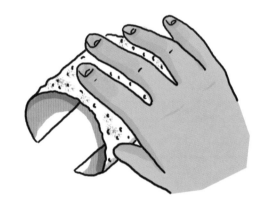

Let dry on a cooling rack and paint.

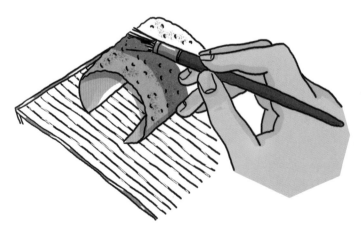

Paper Potpourri

Use paper medallions (page 152) to make a scented ornament. Tuck it into a drawer or closet to keep things smelling sweet.

◤ You will need:

- 2 paper medallions (page 152)
- fresh spices such as whole cloves, freshly grated whole nutmeg, broken pieces of cinnamon stick and/or pieces of vanilla bean
- ribbon 30 cm (12 in.) long
- white glue, hole punch

1 Place a small amount of the spices in the center of one medallion. Make sure the pieces are small.

2 Run glue around the edge of the medallion. Place the second medallion on top, pressing around the edges to secure the glue. Let dry.

3 Punch a hole through the top and pull the ribbon through. Knot or tie in a bow, leaving a loop for hanging, if you like.

Index